MW00937037

Contents

6.78 - 10-12

7 Minor Prophets, Lesson #1

Good Questions Have Small Groups Talking

www.joshhunt.com

Email your group and ask them to do a little reading on the background of Nahum. If they have a Study Bible, they might read the introduction. What a wonderful Bible Study it will be if everyone comes with a little background and knowledge. Another approach is to ask one person to give a little report. Guarantee they will learn more. Also, it is a good way to allow someone to stick their toe in the water of teaching.

Nahum

OPEN

Let's each share your name and what is the next out of town trip you have planned.

DIG

1. **I emailed this week and suggested you read the introduction to Nahum in a Study Bible, if you have one. What did you find out? Someone give us the overview.**

No one likes being in the path of imminent disaster, nor is the menacing threat of enemy invasion a pleasant thought. Can God protect in such circumstances? Will God judge wicked aggressors? Nahum's reply is a clear yes. Nahum's prophecy assures us that God still controls earth's history. His messages are a warning to oppressors and a comfort to the oppressed.

In Nahum's time, the kingdom of Judah was in danger of being swallowed by a great superpower, the Assyrian empire. From Nineveh, the capital, the great king Ashurbanipal (668–626 BC) brought Assyrian might to its zenith. Its military power and cultural influence spanned the length and breadth of the ancient Near East. Even the age-old city of Thebes had felt the conqueror's heel (3:8–10).

The times were less than encouraging for Nahum and the people of Judah. Israel, their sister kingdom to the north, had already fallen to the Assyrians in 722 BC, and Judah now faced the same imperial enemy. To make matters worse, Ashurbanipal had recently captured Judah's king, the wicked Manasseh (697–642 BC), and taken him to Babylon (2 Chr 33:10–11). Following his release from captivity, a repentant Manasseh (2 Chr 33:12–17) attempted to undo his former wickedness (2 Kgs 21:1–18; 2 Chr 33:1–9). Despite his efforts, his prior evil influence still permeated the land. This, coupled with the long shadow of Assyrian supremacy, cast a cloud of doom over God's people. Thus, Nahum's prophetic messages of Nineveh's fall and of hope for Judah's future were timely. — *New Living Translation Study Bible* (Carol Stream, IL: Tyndale House Publishers, Inc., 2008), Na.

2. **Nahum is considered a sequel to the book of Jonah. What do you recall about the book of Jonah?**

Jonah is well-known and loved for the amazing and ironic events it recounts. Although Jonah is the main character, the book's main purpose is not to teach us about him but to teach us about God. Through Jonah's experience, God, the all-powerful Creator, reveals that though he is a God who will pour out his wrath on the wicked, he is also one who eagerly pours out his mercy on those who repent—including those we would too quickly deem to be beyond mercy.

Jonah was a prophet in the northern kingdom of Israel during the politically prosperous but spiritually dark reign of Jeroboam II (793–753 BC). Despite Jeroboam's spiritual failures (see 2 Kgs 14:23–24), God allowed him to continue the expansion of territory begun under his father, King Jehoash. This expansion, predicted by God through Jonah (2 Kgs 14:25, 28), eventually brought Israel's territory back to approximately what it had been in the glory days of David and Solomon (see 1 Kgs 8:65). When Jonah prophesied, nationalistic zeal was running high.

The book of Jonah records the prophet's visit to Nineveh, a key city in the Assyrian empire. Assyria's power had swelled in previous decades. During that time, Shalmaneser III of Assyria (858–824 BC) extended the influence of the empire well into Palestine. Assyrian annals from that period record Shalmaneser confronting the Israelite king Ahab (1 Kgs 17–22), among others, at the famous battle of Qarqar (853 BC). But during the reigns of Jehoash (798–782 BC) and Jeroboam II (793–753 BC) in Israel, Assyria's dominance in the region waned because of failed leadership and continued resistance on the frontiers. Jonah preached in Nineveh when the Assyrian empire was at this low point, probably around 755 BC.

Some years following Jonah's visit to Nineveh, Assyria began reasserting itself throughout the Near East during the reign of Tiglath-pileser III (744–727 BC). In 722 BC, a few decades after Jonah, Assyria sacked Samaria and brought the northern kingdom of Israel to an end. A century later, the prophet

Nahum of Judah announced the imminent destruction of Nineveh and the Assyrian empire for its pervasive wickedness. Nineveh was destroyed by the Babylonians in 612 BC. The repentance brought about through Jonah's preaching evidently took no lasting root. — *New Living Translation Study Bible* (Carol Stream, IL: Tyndale House Publishers, Inc., 2008), Jon.

3. **How is Nahum's message similar to Jonah's? How is it different?**

One hundred years earlier Jonah spoke to Nineveh. Now it was Nahum's turn, and his message was quite different... The prophet Jonah spoke of imminent doom, and the Ninevites repented, saving themselves from God's certain judgment. By the time of Nahum, the Ninevites' sin had become so entrenched that there was no longer any hope of return—and no one to whom they could turn for help.

How terrifying to realize that God is against you! Our God is long-suffering, gracious, and merciful, but He is also thoroughly just. If we do not turn to Him in repentance, He will measure out His justice. He looks past our religious ritual and formulaic prayers and sees our hearts. He knows who genuinely trusts Him, and He will be their unassailable fortress in times of distress.

Jonah and Nahum had messages for Nineveh: Jonah indicated that God will show mercy to those who turn to Him; Nahum revealed that God's judgment must fall on the unrepentant.

Are you truly repentant? Guard your heart lest you become indifferent to God's grace and mercy. — Henry Blackaby and Richard Blackaby, *Discovering God's Daily Agenda* (Nashville: Thomas Nelson, 2007).

4. **A lot of people know the stories of the Bible. What we do not know is the story of the Bible. Let's review this way. I want to give you a pair of names, and you tell me which one came first and how you know:**

David / Daniel

Abraham / Solomon

Nahum / Joseph

Nahum / Jonah

Moses / Nehemiah

Joshua / Saul

Isaac / Nahum

Nahum / Jesus

Nahum / Malachi

Jacob / Jonah

Joseph / Joshua

Samson / Saul

5. Nahum is a prophesy to Nineveh. Locate Nineveh on a map.

New Living Translation Study Bible (Carol Stream, IL: Tyndale House Publishers, Inc., 2008), Na.

6. Nahum 1.2. We normally think of jealousy as a bad thing. What does it mean that God is a jealous God?

God is admittedly a jealous God. He cherishes His people's affections and will tolerate no rivals. He is not content to be a priority in your life; He wants to be the G priority. God demands your exclusive devotion. He does not abide unfaithfulness or attitudes and habits that threaten His place in your heart.

Take a quick inventory. What is competing for God's foremost position in your life? Look at your calendar... Mentally review your financial commitments... What do you see about yourself and about the priority God is in your everyday life? In what ways are you investing in your relationship with the

Lord? Or are you busying yourself in inconsequential activities and earthly pursuits?

Now consider the objects of your devotion. Has your love for someone made that person an idol? Are you longing for riches or the success and security that the world offers? What keeps you from loving God with all your heart, soul, mind, and strength?

God is a jealous God: He wants your devotion. His Spirit can grow that kind of love in your heart. Why not lay your bad attitudes, destructive habits, and false gods at His feet today?
— Henry Blackaby and Richard Blackaby, *Discovering God's Daily Agenda* (Nashville: Thomas Nelson, 2007).

7. **What is great about the fact that God is a jealous God?**

A celebrity talk show host recently told her television audience that she didn't feel right believing in a God who says He is jealous. On the face of it, the statement that God is a jealous God does sound strange.

Jealousy is a powerful emotion. It can devastate relationships and destroy lives. So why would the eternal, sovereign, almighty God name Himself "Jealous"?

When God says He is a jealous God, He is not saying He is jealous of us or of something we have. He is also not saying He is fearful of losing His position in our lives, the way a person might be possessive in a human relationship. What He is saying is that He is jealous for us. We are so precious to Him that He wants the highest and best for us, which can only be found when He is first in our lives. He knows that when we love anyone or anything else more than Him, we harm ourselves and damage our relationship with Him.

The God of the Bible is jealous for our sake. He deserves no less than all our worship. — Ava Pennington, *One Year Alone with God: 366 Devotions on the Names of God* (Grand Rapids, MI: Baker, 2010).

8. **Nahum 1.2 also says that God is an avenging God. How does your translation have that?**

The LORD is a jealous and avenging God; the LORD takes vengeance and is filled with wrath. The LORD takes vengeance on his foes and maintains his wrath against his enemies. Nahum 1:2 (NIV)

GOD is serious business. He won't be trifled with. He avenges his foes. He stands up against his enemies, fierce and raging. Nahum 1:2 (MSG)

God is jealous over those he loves; that is why he takes vengeance on those who hurt them. He furiously destroys their enemies. Nahum 1:2 (TLB)

The LORD is a jealous and avenging God; the LORD takes vengeance and is fierce in wrath. The LORD takes vengeance against His foes; He is furious with His enemies. Nahum 1:2 (HCSB)

The LORD God demands loyalty. In his anger, he takes revenge on his enemies. Nahum 1:2 (CEV)

God does not tolerate rivals. The LORD takes revenge. The LORD takes revenge and is full of anger. The LORD takes revenge against his enemies and holds a grudge against his foes. Nahum 1:2 (GW)

9. What exactly does avenging mean?

From jealousy, vengeance arises: 'The LORD is a jealous and avenging God.' He repays the wicked for their sins, and avenges the blood of his servants (Deuteronomy 32:43). The guilty he does not leave without affliction, but 'punishes the children for the sin of the fathers to the third and fourth generation' (Numbers 14:18). On the appointed day Assyria, that empire of 'endless cruelty' (3:19), will 'be consumed like dry stubble' (1:10) by his fiery wrath. 'It is mine to avenge; I will repay. In due time their foot will slip; their day of disaster is near and their doom rushes upon them' (Deuteronomy 32:35).

The word vengeance (avenging) is repeated three times in this verse, not to draw attention to the Holy Trinity as some commentators suggest, but to amplify and confirm the truth. God's disconsolate people and his carefree enemies must be in no doubt that 'the LORD takes vengeance on his foes'. For the downtrodden such a declaration is a message of hope and inspiration; but for the wicked, it is like a flaming sword that makes their 'bodies tremble' (2:10). — Tim Shenton, *Nahum and Obadiah: An Expositional Commentary, Exploring the Bible Commentary* (Leominster, UK: Day One Publications, 2007), 22.

10. What is great about the fact that God is an avenging God?

Do you ever watch the evening news and think, "How does a loving and just God allow such great evil?" You are not alone. Israel often wondered the same thing, so God sent his prophets to put world events into biblical focus.

The prophet Nahum lived during the fall and destruction of the Assyrian empire, which was assured by the fall of Nineveh in 612 BC. Nahum's name means "consolation," and Israel certainly needed a word of consolation. Assyria was one of the most cruel and ruthless nations of the ancient world. They destroyed and burned cities, then subjected the conquered inhabitants to all manner of indignities.

The prophecy of Nahum assures us that God is not remote and unconcerned when it comes to world events. Nahum begins by a threefold reminder that God is an "avenging God" (verse 2). Yet his anger is not like ours. It is righteous and just. So while he is great in power, he is slow to anger. We are often guilty of mistaking God's patience for a lack of justice. We cry out that God is not fair when we see the guilty going unpunished. Yet the prophet assures the reader—"The Lord will never leave the guilty unpunished" (verse 3).

The prophet goes on to demonstrate God's power over all the earth and its peoples with a simple conclusion: "Who can withstand His indignation? Who can endure His burning anger?" (verse 6). Yet our awesome God is also completely just. He is "good, a stronghold in the day of distress" (verse 7). He knows those who take refuge in him. But a just God cannot leave the guilty unpunished. Thus, Nahum repeats the word of judgment, declaring that God will "completely destroy" Nineveh (verse 8). The capital of godless Assyria would be no more.

We are sometimes guilty of over-sentimentalizing God, suggesting he will not bring judgment or cast sinners into hell. God is just and cannot overlook sin. Yet he is a refuge for those who know him. — Ken Hemphill, *Kingdom Promises: God Will* (Nashville: B&H, 2008).

11. Why is LORD in all caps in this section?

Who is this God that stands up to threaten great Nineveh, and why has he waited so long? Nahum introduces him as "the LORD." The NIV uses all capital letters to indicate that the word Nahum is using is not the normal Hebrew word for "lord" or "master." The word translated as "LORD" is the special, proper name that the Israelites used for their God. Some Bibles use the English equivalents for the Hebrew letters Y(J), H, V(W), H and then write the word in English as Yahweh. The Jews of post-exilic times considered this special name too sacred to speak or pronounce. So whenever they saw it written, they said "Adonai," which is the normal Hebrew word for "master" or "lord."

Several hundred years after the time of Christ, Jewish scholars added vowels to the Hebrew Scriptures. (Up to that time Hebrew words had been written only in consonants.) When they did so, they put the vowels for Adonai under the consonants JHVH, to show how they wanted the word pronounced. If you pronounce the four Hebrew consonants of God's special name with the vowels for Adonai, you come up with the combination Jehovah. This has become a popular name for God among us, but it was never a name that the ancient Israelites or the later Jews used.

The word JHVH comes from the Hebrew verb "to be" and simply means "he is." That was the name by which the Israelites knew God, "HE IS." When God revealed himself to Moses at the burning bush, he used the name in the first person form and identified himself as "I AM WHO I AM" (Exodus 3:14). When the Israelites used this name, they thought of the God who had chosen them and had made a covenant to deal with them in his faithful love.

The name "HE IS" reminded God's people of his sovereign love. Unlike us, God is a being of independent existence and activity. We are and we act because God called us into being, because our parents passed on the gift of life to us, and because conditions on this earth are just right to sustain life. Without these we couldn't exist. God, however, is dependent on no one and nothing. He simply "is"—and he does what "is" wants. If he chose to love Israel and make them his own, the reason simply is because "HE IS," and he is love. — James J. Westendorf, *Nahum, Habakkuk, Zephaniah, The People's Bible* (Milwaukee, WI: Northwestern Pub. House, 2000), 27–29.

12. One more truth we learn about God from verse 2. God is a God of wrath. What is great about serving a God of wrath?

We now come to a topic that is perhaps unpleasant to discuss, but it is essential if we are to have a right understanding of God: His wrath. The idea of a wrathful God goes against the wishful thinking of fallen human nature. Even much evangelism today speaks only of the joys and blessings of salvation without mentioning that those who are without God are under His wrath (Eph. 2:3).

God's attributes are balanced in divine perfection. If He had no righteous anger, He would not be God, just as He would not be God without His gracious love. He perfectly loves righteousness and perfectly hates evil (Ps. 45:7).

But God's wrath isn't like ours. The Greek word used for God's wrath in the New Testament refers to a settled, determined indignation. God does not "fly off the handle," whereas we tend to be emotional and uncontrolled in our anger.

Many times God expressed His wrath to sinful mankind in past ages. He destroyed all mankind except Noah and his family in the great Flood (Gen. 6–7). He destroyed Sodom and Gomorrah for their sins (Gen. 18–19). The Lord told unfaithful Israel, "Behold, My anger and My wrath will be poured out on this place, on man and on beast and on the trees of the field and on the fruit of the ground; and it will burn and not be quenched" (Jer. 7:20).

Some people today foolishly think the God of the Old Testament was a God of wrath and the New Testament God was a God of love, but His wrath is just as clearly taught in the New Testament. Jesus says, "He who believes in the Son has eternal life; but he who does not obey the Son shall not see life, but the wrath of God abides on him" (John 3:36). In the end–times Jesus will return "dealing out retribution to those who do not know God and to those who do not obey the gospel of our Lord Jesus" (2 Thess. 1:8). God is the same God, and He will always hate sin. — John MacArthur, *Strength for Today* (Wheaton, IL: Crossway Books, 1997).

13. Some people say that the God of the Old Testament is a God of wrath, where the God of the New Testament is a God of mercy. Is this right?

Too many people talk about God being a God of wrath in the Old Testament and a God of love and peace in the New Testament. But God is the same throughout the Bible.

It is true that the Old Testament tells us God is holy and pure, and He punishes those who rebel against Him. But the New Testament tells us the same thing. In fact, some of the strongest warnings about judgment in the Bible come from the lips of Jesus (see Matthew 7:14).

In the same way, the New Testament certainly stresses God's love and mercy. In fact, it gives us the greatest proof that God loves us: Jesus laid down His life for our salvation (1 John 3:16). But the Old Testament also tells us repeatedly about God's love for us: "I have loved you with an everlasting love; I have drawn you with loving kindness" (Jeremiah 31:3).

Still not convinced? Then consider this an invitation to open the pages of the Bible for yourself. You'll be blessed as you get to know God more fully—in all of His righteousness and love. — Billy Graham, *Wisdom for Each Day* (Nashville: Thomas Nelson, 2008).

14. I read one writer who said God could not be a God of love unless He was also a God of wrath. What do you think he meant by that?

The Bible presents a God who is the absolute of perfection, who is a God of love, and yet who is simultaneously a God of wrath. A. T. Pierson compares it to an arch. You have the love of God supporting one side and the wrath of God supporting the other side, and without either of them the entire thing would fall down.

God would not be God if he didn't have the capacity of wrath. Why? I was reading the other day about a young, handsome, dapper fellow, a medical doctor, who always wore crisp and well-tailored clothing. He handled himself with polish and smoothness. He always bore the fragrance of expensive cologne. But his very demeanor made him all the more fiendish, for his name was Josef Mengele, the Angel of Death at Auschwitz. With a flick of his well-washed and perfumed hand he personally selected 400,000 prisoners to die in the gas chamber. He conducted horrible experiments on people, hoping to produce a superior race. One observer said, "He would spend hours bent over his microscope while the air outside stank with the heavy odor of burning flesh from the chimney stacks of the crematoria."

He had a special fascination for children who were twins. He would give them horrible injections, operate on their spine to paralyze them, then begin removing parts of their body one at a time for observation.

Now, what would you think of a person—or, for that matter, a God—who could see that sort of indescribable evil without feeling any anger? If God could watch the hurt and the evil in this universe with no feelings of indignation and fury, he would be defective in his character. He wouldn't be God at all.

So I submit that rather than apologizing for the doctrine of the wrath of God, or ignoring it, we should appreciate it as a vital and wonderful part of God's divine character. — Robert J. Morgan, *Nelson's Complete Book of Stories, Illustrations, and Quotes, electronic ed.* (Nashville: Thomas Nelson Publishers, 2000), 502.

15. We talk a lot about having a personal relationship with God. How can we have a personal relationship with a God of wrath? How can we get close to an angry God?

God is a God of wrath. But the wrath due to be poured out on all mankind, Christ took on Himself. That's what the apostle Paul meant when he said that those who put their faith in Him have been "justified by His blood" and are assured of being "saved from the wrath of God through [Christ]" (Rom. 5:9). As a result of Christ's atoning work, all Christians are identified with Christ, are adopted as God's children through Him, and are no longer "children of wrath" (Eph. 2:3).

But Paul doesn't stop there because the ongoing intercessory work of Christ has great significance for every believer and the security of his salvation. In Romans 5:10 Paul argues from the greater to the lesser to show that it was a much greater work of God to bring sinners to grace than to bring them to glory. Since God brought us to Himself when we were enemies, we will be reconciled continually now that we are His friends. When God first reconciled us, we were wretched, vile, and godless sinners. Since that was not a barrier to His reconciling us then, there is nothing that can prevent the living Christ from keeping us reconciled.

This truth has great ramifications for our assurance. If God already secured our deliverance from sin, death, and future judgment, how could our present spiritual life possibly be in jeopardy? How can a Christian, whose past and future salvation are guaranteed by God, be insecure in the intervening time? If sin in the greatest degree could not prevent our becoming reconciled, how can sin in lesser degree prevent our staying reconciled? Our salvation can't be any more secure than that. — John MacArthur, *Strength for Today* (Wheaton, IL: Crossway Books, 1997).

16. What do we learn about God from verse 7?

Did you think Jesus only cares about things like heaven and hell? About forgiveness and sin? About holiness and wickedness? About truth and lies? About salvation and judgment? Jesus does care about those things. But He also cares about your job, about whether your child makes the sports team, about your children's college tuition, about your budget now that you're unexpectedly pregnant, about the roof that leaks, about the cranky transmission in the car, and about all the other physical problems and needs we face.

Jesus cares even if the physical problem we face is largely of our own making. He cares if we are having car trouble, even if it was caused by our not having taken the time to change the oil regularly.... Jesus cares about your physical needs today. —ANNE GRAHAM LOTZ, from *Just Give Me Jesus* / Thomas Nelson, *A Daybook of Prayer: Meditations, Scriptures and Prayers to Draw near to the Heart of God* (Nashville: Thomas Nelson, 2006).

17. What is a refuge? What does it mean that God is our refuge?

The words used in verse 7 are a welcome reminder of the unchanging goodness of Yahweh, even in the midst of horrific judgment. This verse stands as a light in the midst of the darkness of Nahum's oracle. Preceded by "rocks are shattered before him" and followed by "with an overwhelming flood he will make an end," the goodness of Yahweh is not forgotten. This would have been a word of hope to any believers living in Nineveh as well as to Judah. The ultimate terms of relationship to the good Lord Creator are set in the sharpest contrast possible: Either he is a trust and a refuge, or he is opposed and a pursuer of those opponents.

God's goodness is declared in three phrases that have familiar uses in other biblical texts (Nah. 1:7). "The LORD is good" is often used in the context of suffering or reaping consequences of rebellion against the Creator (Ps. 34:7–8; 145:8–10; Jer. 33:10–11; Lam. 3:21–26). "The LORD is a refuge in times of trouble" is used in Psalm 9:9; 46:1; 62:8; and Joel 3:16. "Refuge" often means a safe place of hiding from an enemy. "He cares for those who trust [ḥasah] in him"; ḥasah is often used to express "find[ing] refuge in the shadow of your wings" (Ps. 36:7; 57:1; see also 2 Sam. 22:31;

Ps. 18:30; Prov. 30:5). — James Bruckner, *Jonah, Nahum, Habakkuk, Zephaniah, The NIV Application Commentary* (Grand Rapids, MI: Zondervan Publishing House, 2004), 149.

18. We always want to read the Bible for application. What is the application of verse 7 to our daily lives?

Take your problems promptly to God. He could help you much faster if you were not so slow in turning to prayer, but you try everything else first.

Now that you have caught your breath and your trouble has passed, recuperate in God's mercies. God is near you to repair all damage and to make things better than before. Is anything too hard for God? Where is your faith? Stand strong in God. Have patience and courage. Comfort will come in time. Wait. He will come to you with healing.

Are you anxious about the future? What will that gain you but sorrow? "Do not worry about tomorrow, for tomorrow will worry about itself. Each day has enough trouble of its own" (Matthew 6:34).

...When you think you are far from God, he is really quite near. When you feel that all is lost, sometimes the greatest gain is ready to be yours. Don't judge everything by the way you feel right now. If, for a while, you feel no comfort from God, he has not rejected you. He has set you on the road to the kingdom of heaven. —THOMAS À KEMPIS / Thomas Nelson, *A Daybook of Prayer: Meditations, Scriptures and Prayers to Draw near to the Heart of God* (Nashville: Thomas Nelson, 2006).

19. What did you learn today that you want to take with you?

20. How can we support one another in prayer this week?

7 Minor Prophets, Lesson #2

Good Questions Have Small Groups Talking

www.joshhunt.com

When is the last time you had a class fellowship? You can double your class in two years or less by inviting every member and every prospect to every fellowship every month. A group of 10 that doubles every 18 months will reach 1000 people in 10 years.

Zephaniah 1, 2

OPEN

Let's each share your name and one thing you are grateful for this week.

DIG

1. **Who has a Study Bible? What is the overview of Zephaniah?**

   We have a word for people who predict terrible times ahead: doomsayer. It's an unflattering word, meant to poke fun at the bearers of bad news. We don't really want to believe their predictions of doom, so we caricature them. Maybe they will feel ashamed and go away. Sometimes it helps a little when the prophet of doom offers a solution. The unspoken question "Is there any hope?" is on everyone's mind.

Zephaniah's message had both halves of the bad-news-goodnews equation. His first words were bad news indeed: the day of the Lord was coming and that meant terrible judgment. The Israelites had acted like their pagan neighbors—they had scorned God's law, worshiped false gods, and sinned without remorse long enough. Now it was time to repent: they had to turn back to their God or face the consequences.

It was the "turn back to God" part of Zephaniah's message that offered a ray of hope. And to those who listened and responded to his call, the good news wiped out every line of bad. God would restore those who sought Him. — Earl D. Radmacher, Ronald Barclay Allen, and H. Wayne House, *The Nelson Study Bible: New King James Version* (Nashville: T. Nelson Publishers, 1997), Zep.

2. About what was the date for Zephaniah? Where did he minister?

History tells us that it worked. The Book of Zephaniah tells about events that took place in the city of Jerusalem in the late seventh century B.C., when Josiah was king. The northern kingdom Israel had been destroyed nearly a century earlier by the Assyrians. The southern kingdom Judah had suffered under the extraordinarily wicked rules of Manasseh (697–642 B.C.) and Amon (642–640 B.C.). The evils of their reigns had made doom appear certain. But the godly King Josiah led an important revival that affected all Judah. Scripture reports that this revival, though short-lived, delayed God's judgment, the invasion by Babylon (2 Chr. 34:27, 28).

Zephaniah's message announced the day of the Lord—a coming day of doom—in the darkest of terms, but it also promised the blessing of future glory in a picture as bright as the doom was dark.

Author and Date • The prophet Zephaniah traced his ancestry back four generations to Hezekiah, most likely Judah's famous king. After the long and evil reign of Manasseh (697–642 B.C.) and his son Amon (642–640 B.C.), Josiah began his rule of Judah. Zephaniah began ministering as prophet in Jerusalem in the same year as the great prophet Jeremiah (627 B.C.). They and Hulda the prophetess (see 2 Chr. 34:14–28) witnessed the religious reform that Josiah started, a reform that unfortunately did not last. After Josiah's death, the people returned to their errant ways; less than fifty years later (around 586 B.C.), God used Babylon to discipline them. — Earl D. Radmacher, Ronald Barclay Allen, and H. Wayne House, *The Nelson Study Bible: New King James Version* (Nashville: T. Nelson Publishers, 1997), Zep.

3. **Let's review the story of the Old Testament. I have 4 strings of names on the board. Let's work on putting each string in chronological order. (I will have them in Chronological order below; mix them up when you put them on the board.)**

Adam, Abraham, Moses, David

Cain, Isaac, Joshua, Saul

Tower of Babel, Jacob, Solomon, Nehemiah

Noah, Deborah, Zephaniah, Malachi

Zephaniah, Daniel, Nehemiah, Malachi

4. **One more background/ context question. Zephaniah ministered at the same time as Jeremiah. What do you recall about Jeremiah? How were they similar? How were they different?**

Although Zephaniah and Jeremiah delivered the same message at the same time to the same people, the two men couldn't have been more different in temperament. Jeremiah was a poet, a lamenter, the "weeping prophet." He delivered his message like a skilled harpist—playing the minor melody of judgment as tears coursed down his cheeks. Not Zephaniah. If Jeremiah played a harp, surely Zephaniah wielded a hammer. He held nothing back as he delivered God's message with relentless force and power.

Yet God used them both. Today, the Lord has a plan custom-made for you. When you hear or see someone whose ministry has a different flavor than yours, don't feel like you have to duplicate his style—for regardless of whether you feel more comfortable gripping a hammer or plucking a harp, God will use you just as He has made you.

Like that of so many Old Testament prophets, Zephaniah's message was twofold as it concerned not only the situation of his day but of a day yet to come. The word of the Lord given to Zephaniah was a word of judgment, with verses 2 through 4 detailing who God would judge and verses 5 and 6 explaining why He would judge. — Jon Courson, *Jon Courson's Application Commentary: Volume Two: Psalms-Malachi* (Nashville, TN: Thomas Nelson, 2006), 870–871.

5. **Verse 1. Do you recognize any of Zephaniah's ancestors?**

Other prophets either neglect to mention their genealogies altogether or they record two or three generations at the most. Not Zephaniah. He opened his book by tracing his lineage four generations—all the way back to his great-great grandfather, Hizkiah—or, as we know him, Hezekiah. This gives us a possible clue as to why Zephaniah recorded his family tree so carefully. Perhaps, under the inspiration of the Spirit, he wanted to make it known that he was related to royalty, that he was the great-great grandson of one of the greatest kings of Judah. — Jon Courson, *Jon Courson's Application Commentary: Volume Two: Psalms-Malachi* (Nashville, TN: Thomas Nelson, 2006), 871.

6. **2 Kings 18. Did Hezekiah reign in the Northern Kingdom, or Southern Kingdom?**

HEZEKIAH Son and successor of Ahaz as king of Judah (716/15–687/86 B.C.). Hezekiah began his reign when he was 25 years old. At this time in history, the nation of Assyria had risen to power.

King Hezekiah's tunnel that brought water from the Gihon Spring to the pool of Siloam.

Hezekiah began his reign by bringing religious reform to Judah. Hezekiah was not willing to court the favor of the Assyrian kings. The temple in Jerusalem was reopened. The idols were removed from the temple. Temple vessels that had been desecrated during Ahaz's reign were sanctified for use in the temple. The sacrifices were initiated with singing and the sounds of musical instruments. The tribes in the Northern Kingdom (Israel) had been subjected to Assyrian dominance. Hezekiah invited the Israelites to join in the celebration of the Passover in Jerusalem. Places of idol worship were destroyed. Hezekiah even destroyed the bronze serpent Moses had erected in the wilderness (Num. 21:4–9) so the people would not view the bronze serpent as an object of worship. Hezekiah organized the priests and Levites for the conducting of religious services. The tithe was reinstituted. Plans were made to observe the religious feasts called for in the Law. — Gary Hardin, "Hezekiah," ed. Chad Brand et al., *Holman Illustrated Bible Dictionary* (Nashville, TN: Holman Bible Publishers, 2003), 757–758.

7. 2 Kings 18.9 – 12. What momentous event happened in the North (Israel) during Hezekiah's reign in the South (Judah)?

In 725, Shalmaneser began to besiege Samaria, but then he died (or was killed) and his leading general, Sargon II, took over. The siege lasted three years, and in 722, the city capitulated. Assyria had already taken the tribes east of the Jordan (1 Chron. 5:24–26), so now they possessed everything but Judah, and that would fall to Babylon.

Israel lost its land (v. 6; 18:9–12). As we have seen, Assyria's policy was to relocate conquered peoples and replace them with prisoners from other nations. It was clearly stated in God's covenant with His people that their disobedience would bring defeat in war (Deut. 28:25, 49–50, 52), oppression and slavery (Deut. 28:29, 33, 48, 68), and captivity (Deut. 28:36, 43, 63–68); and all of this happened to both Israel and Judah. The land belonged to the Lord (Lev. 25:2, 23, 38) and the people were His "tenants." Not only was the land His, but so were the people (Lev. 25:55). They would possess the land and enjoy its blessings as long as they kept the terms of the covenant, but repeated disobedience would bring discipline within the land and ultimately discipline outside the land. That's exactly what happened. Because of the people's sins during the period of the judges, seven different nations invaded the land, took the crops, and enslaved the people right in their own land. After the division of the nation, Israel was taken captive by Assyria and Judah by Babylon. God kept the terms of His covenant. — Warren W. Wiersbe, *Be Distinct, "Be" Commentary Series* (Colorado Springs, CO: Victor, 2002), 115–116.

8. 2 Kings 18.15 – 16. How was the South (Judah) affected by Assyria's conquest of Israel?

A chapter earlier the writer told us how Samaria was captured and how the ten northern tribes were carried into captivity because of their continued impenitence. By repeating those facts here, the writer shows us how the piety of King Hezekiah stood in sharp contrast to the attitude of others and how God protects all who trust in his mercy.

Ten years after Samaria fell, the mighty Assyrian armies invaded Palestine again. Sennacherib easily captured the fortified cities around Jerusalem. He was now encamped at Lachish, an imposing fortress some 20 miles southwest of Jerusalem. Humanly speaking, nothing would stop him from capturing Jerusalem and Egypt as well. — Arno J. Wolfgramm, Kings, *The People's Bible* (Milwaukee, WI: Northwestern Pub. House, 1990), 267–268.

9. 2 Kings 19. How was it that Judah didn't suffer the same fate as Israel?

King Hezekiah expressed his grief by tearing his clothes. By putting on sackcloth he expressed his sorrow over the sins of his own people.

But Hezekiah did not despair. This king, whose faith was unlike that of any other king (18:5), took the matter to the Lord. He not only came to the temple; he also sent messengers to Isaiah the prophet, who was now an old man, and asked him to intercede on behalf of God's people. With the powerful Assyrian army at their gates, God's people were like a woman in labor who suddenly loses her strength and is unable to give birth. Now that the ten northern tribes had been carried away into captivity, now that even the walled cities of Judah had fallen, God's people in Jerusalem were but a small remnant.

Jesus has told us, "Everyone who exalts himself will be humbled, and he who humbles himself will be exalted" (Luke 18:14). That is what happened here. God heard Hezekiah's humble prayer of faith and promised that the arrogant Assyrian would be struck down.

Hezekiah is a good example for us. God's people today also face problems and difficulties that nearly overwhelm us. But when we call out to God, when we seek comfort, strength, and direction from God's prophets, we will never be disappointed. With the poet, we sing, "Preserve, O Lord, thine honor, the bold blasphemer smite" (TLH 264:2). — Arno J. Wolfgramm, Kings, *The People's Bible* (Milwaukee, WI: Northwestern Pub. House, 1990), 272–273.

10. How do you think Hezekiah was remembered? What was his legacy? When Zephaniah mentions him, what feelings come to mind for the people back in the day?

IN CONTRAST TO all the previous kings of Israel and Judah, Hezekiah is introduced as the faithful king, one who reformed Judean worship and moved Judah toward the ideal of the covenant. Hezekiah is not merely similar to David as Asa (1 Kings 15:11) or Jehoshaphat (22:43) were, but is the very model of the Davidic ideal (2 Kings 18:3, 5). His faithfulness results in the preservation of Jerusalem, a stark contrast to the captivity of Israel. — August H. Konkel, *1 & 2 Kings, The NIV Application Commentary* (Grand Rapids, MI: Zondervan, 2006), 598.

11. Do a search for Josiah. What do we know about him?

The period when Zephaniah was given his message is described as being during the reign of Josiah son of Amon king of Judah. That, however, covers a 31 year period from 640 to 609 BC (2 Kings 22:1), and so the question arises as to whether it was early or late in Josiah's reign that Zephaniah's ministry fell. His prophecy of the destruction of the Assyrian Empire and its capital Nineveh (2:13–15) must have occurred before that city fell in 612 BC, and so it was in the earlier part of Josiah's reign that he was active.

There are two key events within that period: the twelfth year of Josiah's reign (628 BC) when he began to purge Judah and Jerusalem of idolatry (2 Chron. 34:3) and the eighteenth year (622 BC) when the Book of the Law was found in the course of renovation work on the Temple and gave the impetus for further major reforms (2 Chron. 34:8–33). The description Zephaniah gives of conditions in Jerusalem points to a time before Josiah's reforming activities of 622, and may well predate his earlier reforms of 628. Since it is recorded that when Josiah was sixteen he 'began to seek the God of his father David' (2 Chron. 34:3), it is possible to view Zephaniah's ministry as influencing the course of Josiah's activity. At the latest Zephaniah had begun his ministry by the time Jeremiah was called to the prophetic office in the thirteenth year of Josiah's reign (Jer. 1:2).

That means that Zephaniah was active before Habakkuk even though Habakkuk's prophecy precedes his in the Old Testament. The factors which influenced the ancient scribes in their arrangement of the twelve minor prophets are not totally clear. Chronology played some part. Hosea and Amos are generally agreed to be among the oldest of the Twelve and they are placed at the beginning, just as the post-exilic prophets, Haggai, Zechariah and Malachi, are placed at the end. But Amos prophesied before Hosea though the book of Hosea comes first in the canonical order. Perhaps the fact that Hosea was longer was viewed as significant. Here I think Zephaniah is placed after Habakkuk for thematic reasons. Zephaniah's concluding vision of God in the midst of his people was deliberately placed before Haggai's prophecy which deals with the rebuilding of the Temple, the first stage in the realisation of Zephaniah's prophecy. — John L. MacKay, *Jonah, Micah, Nahum, Habakkuk and Zephaniah, Focus on the Bible Commentary* (Ross-shire, Great Britain: Christian Focus Publications, 1998), 332–333.

12. 2 Chronicles 34. What good things did Josiah do?

Josiah was only 8 years old when he became king. Evidently he had spiritually motivated advisers or regents; by the time he was 16 he began of his own accord "to seek the God of David" (2 Chr 34:3). When he was 20, he became greatly exercised over the idolatry of the land and launched a major effort to eradicate the pagan high places, groves, and images from Judah and Jerusalem. So intense was Josiah's hatred of idolatry that he even opened the tombs of pagan priests and burned their bones on pagan altars before these were destroyed.

Josiah carried his reform movement beyond the borders of Judah, venting his fury especially on the cult center at Bethel, where Jeroboam had set up his false worship. In fulfillment of prophecy (1 Kgs 13:1–3), he destroyed the altar and high place and burned the bones of officiating priests to desecrate the Site (2 Kgs 23:15–18). What he did at Bethel, he did everywhere else in the kingdom of Samaria (2 Kgs 23:19, 20). — Walter A. Elwell and Barry J. Beitzel, *Baker Encyclopedia of the Bible* (Grand Rapids, MI: Baker Book House, 1988), 1223.

13. 2 Chronicles 34.14 is a shocking verse to me. How could they have lost the Bible?

When Josiah was 26, he launched a project to cleanse and repair the temple in Jerusalem (2 Kgs 22:3). Shaphan, the king's administrative assistant, commissioned the work; Hilkiah the priest exercised direct supervision of renovation and construction. In the process of restoring the temple, Hilkiah found the book of the law, the nature and contents of which are otherwise unknown. Possibly in the dark days of Manasseh a deliberate attempt had been made to destroy the Word of God. At any rate, evidently there was little knowledge of Scripture in Judah. — Walter A. Elwell and Barry J. Beitzel, *Baker Encyclopedia of the Bible* (Grand Rapids, MI: Baker Book House, 1988), 1223.

14. What difference did discovering and reading the Bible make?

When Shaphan read the book of the law to Josiah, the king was devastated by the pronouncements of judgment against apostasy contained in it; he sent a delegation to Huldah the prophetess to find out what judgments awaited the land. The prophetess replied that the condemnation of God would indeed fall on Judah for its sin, but sent word to Josiah that because his heart was right toward God, the punishment would not come during his lifetime.

The king called together a large representative group for a public reading of the law—evidently sections especially concerned with obligations to God. The king and the people covenanted before God to keep his commandments.

Faced with the importance of maintaining a pure monotheistic faith, the king was spurred on to even more rigorous efforts to cleanse the temple and Jerusalem. He destroyed the vessels used in Baal worship, the monument of horses and chariot of the sun given by the kings of Judah for sun worship, the homosexual community near the temple, and shrines built by Solomon and in use since his day. Moreover, he made stringent efforts to eliminate the pagan shrines and high places in all the towns of Judah (2 Kgs 23:4–14). — Walter A. Elwell and Barry J. Beitzel, *Baker Encyclopedia of the Bible* (Grand Rapids, MI: Baker Book House, 1988), 1223.

15. How does Zephaniah's message relate to this reform?

Zephaniah prophesied during the reign of King Josiah (meaning "the LORD supports"). Josiah came to the throne as a boy after the fifty-five-year reign of evil Manasseh and the futile two-year reign of Amon (which ended in assassination by servants). Josiah's good and productive thirty-one-year reign was guided by the discovery of the book of Deuteronomy in the eighteenth year of his reign during a remodeling of the temple (2 Kings 21:24–23:30; 2 Chron. 33:25–35:27). His reform of the corruption of wealth and worship in Jerusalem (also Zephaniah's subject matter) delayed Yahweh's judgment pronounced by Zephaniah. Hulda the prophetess confirmed Zephaniah's word that the day of Yahweh (the Babylonian onslaught) would come indeed, but it would be delayed because of Josiah's humility before God (2 Kings 22:20).

Zephaniah's words are related to that reform in some way. Perhaps his preaching preceded the reform and called people to participate: "Gather together, gather together, O shameful nation" (Zeph. 2:1). His words may also have been unwelcome by some in the reform movement, for his radical message of destruction did not explicitly offer a reprieve through repentance (see, e.g., 1:2–3). Reformers usually offer the hope of a better (immediate) future as an incentive to reform, but Zephaniah offers none of this. He only offers hope for a future generation ("daughter of Zion," 3:14; cf. also 3:10). — James Bruckner, *Jonah, Nahum, Habakkuk, Zephaniah, The NIV Application Commentary* (Grand Rapids, MI: Zondervan Publishing House, 2004), 283–284.

16. Verse 2ff. What is Zephaniah's essential message?

The first picture is that of a devastating universal flood (Zeph. 1:2–3). The Hebrew word translated "consume" in the KJV means "to sweep away completely." The picture is that of total devastation of all that God created and is probably a reference to Noah's flood. (You find similar wording in Gen. 6:7; 7:4; 9:8–10.) God gave man dominion over the fish, the fowls, and the beasts (1:28; Ps. 8:7–8), but man lost that dominion when Adam disobeyed God. However, through Jesus Christ, man's lost dominion will one day be restored (Heb. 2:5–9).

God will not only destroy His creation, but He will also destroy the idols that people worship—the "stumbling blocks" that offend the Lord (Ezek. 14:1–8). In Zephaniah's day, idolatry was rife in Judah, thanks to the evil influence of King Manasseh. When God stretches out His hand, it means that judgment is coming (Isa. 9:12, 17, 21). The prophet names two of the false gods that had captured the hearts of the people: Baal, the rain god of the Canaanites (Zeph. 1:4), and Malcom (Milcom, Molech), the terrible god of the Ammonites (1 Kings 11:33; Amos 5:26). The people also worshiped the host of heaven (Deut. 4:19; Jer. 19:13; 32:29) and followed the godless example of the idolatrous priests ("Chemarim" in Zeph. 1:4; see 2 Kings 23:5, 8; Hosea 10:5).

These idolaters may have claimed that they were still faithfully worshiping Jehovah, the true and living God, but Jehovah will not share worship or glory with any other god. In turning to idols, the people had turned away from the Lord and were not seeking Him or His blessing (Zeph. 1:6). They were guilty of sins of commission (worshiping idols) and omission (ignoring the Lord). — Warren W. Wiersbe, *Be Concerned, "Be" Commentary Series* (Colorado Springs, CO: Chariot Victor, 1996), 122–123.

17. Did it happen? Was Judah swept away?

So why does Zephaniah begin with such an absolute statement as, "I cut off man from the face of the earth" (1:3b)? This dramatic beginning has a strong rhetorical effect in Zephaniah's preaching. The book's prophecy is dark, and this beginning prepares the hearer for the difficult words to come and inclines them to listen for hope. It is more than rhetorical, however, for it tells the truth about the horror that will indeed descend on the whole known earth. Babylon will obliterate the land. — James Bruckner, *Jonah, Nahum, Habakkuk, Zephaniah, The NIV Application Commentary* (Grand Rapids, MI: Zondervan Publishing House, 2004), 286.

18. Why did God sweep away Judah? What did it accomplish?

During the Babylonian Captivity, the Jews were cured of their fascination with foreign gods. Their temple was destroyed, their priesthood was scattered, and for seventy years they could not worship the way Moses had commanded them. When they were finally allowed to return to their land, one of the first things the Jews did was rebuild their temple and restore the sacrifices. — Warren W. Wiersbe, *Be Concerned, "Be" Commentary Series* (Colorado Springs, CO: Chariot Victor, 1996), 123.

19. What do we learn about God from Zephaniah's message?

As we see in the history of Israel and in our own life, our long-suffering God is merciful and patient despite His people's continual rebellion. God's love for His people, however, compels Him to hate that which destroys us, so He abhors sin. The reality is that those who reject His love and cling to their sin must face His overwhelming wrath.

"All the earth shall be devoured with the fire of My jealousy," God proclaims through Zephaniah (3:8). God's purposes require Him to discipline and even judge His people. Are you willing to undergo the disciplinary pruning process until God has purged you of your sin?

Remember that the purpose of God's discipline is to purify you so you can enjoy fellowship with Him who loves you dearly. He longs to care for you and comfort you, and He rejoices when you seek Him.

One more thing. You are not one of faceless, nameless millions. He knows you personally. He loves you and celebrates your love for Him. His wrath is simply the response of His holiness to lethal sin that will destroy you. — Henry Blackaby and Richard Blackaby, *Discovering God's Daily Agenda* (Nashville: Thomas Nelson, 2007).

20. What is the application of this message for us?

People have heard this message of judgement down through the centuries, and they still need to realize that they are in danger of God's condemnation that is coming upon the whole world. This is why we, like the apostles, preach the gospel of saving grace to everyone who will listen to God's call to turn aside from sin and turn to Christ in repentance and faith. It should be the aim of every church's social and evangelistic activity to bring sinners face to face with the danger of God's judgement and so help them to turn to the only hope of salvation: faith in the Lord Jesus Christ. — Michael Bentley, *Opening up Zephaniah, Opening Up Commentary* (Leominster: Day One Publications, 2008), 16.

21. How can we support one another in prayer this week?

7 Minor Prophets, Lesson #3

Good Questions Have Small Groups Talking

www.joshhunt.com

When is the last time you had a class fellowship? You can double your class in two years or less by inviting every member and every prospect to every fellowship every month. A group of 10 that doubles every 18 months will reach 1000 people in 10 years.

Zephaniah 3

OPEN

Let's each share your name and one thing you love about following God.

DIG

1. **Refresh our memory. What is the background on Zephaniah? When? Where?**

   Zephaniah is dated during the reign of king Josiah (1:1), who became king of Judah at age eight in 640 B.C. He began to "seek the God of his father David" eight years later and four years after that began a spiritual reformation of the land, in about 628 B.C. (2 Chr. 34:3). The reformation became more fervent in 621 when the "book of the law" was discovered in the temple (2 Chr. 34:8–33). Zephaniah was probably a major influence on the young king (see 1:4–5; see also the introduction to Nahum) and hence predates the reforms. If the "Hezekiah" who is listed as Zephaniah's ancestor is the king by that name, that would explain the book's tracing Zephaniah's ancestry to four generations. His family connections would have given him access to the king.

Message and Purpose. Indictment: Zephaniah's focus is on the city of Jerusalem, which is characterized in 3:1 by oppression, rebellion, and defilement. Furthermore, it is said to be devoid of any faith in the Lord (3:2; see 1:12). The corruption of their leaders receives special attention in 3:3–4. Judah was also practicing an apostate religion, attempting to mix pagan elements with worship of the Lord (1:4–6).

Instruction: First, Zephaniah calls for his hearers to cease their empty and adulterous affirmations of faith (1:5) and submit to the Lord in silent humility and fear ("be silent" in 1:7). Second, he calls for them to gather in humble and prayerful repentance to "seek the Lord" (2:1–3). Third, God commands those who respond appropriately to the first two exhortations (3:8) to "wait for me." In the midst of human sin believers should not lose heart. They should look confidently for the culmination of God's purifying work, when the remnant will call upon Him and serve Him "shoulder to shoulder" (3:9). — David S. Dockery et al., *Holman Bible Handbook* (Nashville, TN: Holman Bible Publishers, 1992), 490.

2. We want to review the story of the Old Testament. Which of these people came first?

Moses / David
Joseph / Zephaniah
Nehemiah /Zephaniah
Sarah / Joshua
Abel / Abraham
Jacob / Joel
Ruth / Rehoboam
Solomon / Zephaniah
Joseph / Samuel

3. **James Boice finds four sins in this passage. See if you can find all four.**

The indictment is an old story by now. Verse 2 of chapter 3 lists four faults of God's people: (1) they obeyed no one, certainly not God; (2) because they obeyed no one, they certainly did not accept correction; (3) they did not trust God; and (4) naturally they did not draw close to the God they distrusted. As God's people they should have done precisely the opposite, but they were as vain as Moab and Ammon, and as arrogant as Nineveh. Verses 3 and 4 carry the indictment further, implicating the leaders. Jerusalem's officials are condemned as "roaring lions." Her rulers are described as "evening wolves." The prophets are "arrogant" and "treacherous." The priests "profane the sanctuary and do violence to the law." What can be done with a people like this? The Lord has done no wrong (v. 5). He even warns of judgment, reminding Judah of other peoples he has destroyed (v. 6). Judah has even seen God's judgment fall on Israel to the north, and still it persists in its ways. What more could God do? — *Boice Expositional Commentary - An Expositional Commentary – The Minor Prophets, Volume 2: Micah-Malachi.*

4. **Zephaniah 3.1. Woe is an old word. What does it mean?**

"Woe to me!" I cried. "I am ruined! For I am a man of unclean lips, and I live among a people of unclean lips, and my eyes have seen the King, the LORD Almighty." (Isaiah 6:5, NIV)

The doors of the temple were not the only things that were shaking. The thing that quaked the most in the building was the body of Isaiah. When he saw the living God, the reigning monarch of the universe displayed before his eyes in all of His holiness, Isaiah cried out, "Woe is me!"

The cry of Isaiah sounds strange to the modern ear. It is rare that we hear people today use the word woe. Since this word is old-fashioned and archaic, some modern translators have preferred to substitute another word in its place. That is a serious mistake. The word woe is a crucial biblical word that we cannot afford to ignore. It has a special meaning.

When we think of woes we think of the troubles encountered in melodramas set in the old-time nickelodians. "The Perils of Pauline" showed the heroine wringing her hands in anguish as the heartless landlord came to foreclose on her mortgage. Or we think of Mighty Mouse flying from his cloud to streak to the rescue of his girlfriend, who is being tied to the railroad tracks by Oilcan Harry. She cries, "Woe is me!" Or we think of the favorite expression of the distraught Kingfish in "The Amos and Andy Show" who said, "Woe is me, Andy, what is I gonna do?"

The term woe has gone the way of other worn-out exclamations like alas or alack or forsooth. The only language that has kept the expression in current usage is Yiddish. The modern Jew still declares his frustrations by exclaiming "Oy vay!" which is a shortened version of the full expression oy vay ist mer. Oy vay is Yiddish for "Oh woe," an abbreviation for the full expression, "Oh woe is me!"

The full force of Isaiah's exclamation must be seen against the background of a special form of speech found in the Bible. When prophets announced their messages, the most frequent form the divine utterances took was the oracle. The oracles were announcements from God that could be good news, or bad news. The positive oracles were prefaced by the word blessed. When Jesus preached the Sermon on the Mount, He used the form of the oracle, saying, "Blessed are the poor in spirit," "Blessed are those who mourn," "Blessed are those who hunger and thirst." His audience understood that He was using the formula of the prophet, the oracle that brought good tidings.

Jesus also used the negative form of the oracle. When He spoke out in angry denunciation of the Pharisees, He pronounced the judgment of God upon their heads by saying to them, "Woe unto you, scribes and Pharisees, hypocrites!" He said this so often that it began to sound like litany. On the lips of a prophet the word woe is an announcement of doom. In the Bible, cities are doomed, nations are doomed, individuals are doomed—all by uttering the oracle of woe.

Isaiah's use of woe was extraordinary. When he saw the Lord, he pronounced the judgment of God upon himself. "Woe to me!" he cried, calling down the curse of God, the utter anathema of judgment and doom upon his own head. It was one thing for a prophet to curse another person in the name of God; it was quite another for a prophet to put that curse upon himself. — R. C. Sproul, *The Holiness of God* (Wheaton, IL: Tyndale House Publishers, 1993).

5. **Verse 2. Zephaniah's complaint was that the people did not draw near to God. Can you think of some other verses that speak of drawing near to God? Do a search on your smart phone if you have one.**

Hebrews 7:19 (for the law made nothing perfect), and a better hope is introduced, by which we draw near to God.

Hebrews 7:25 Therefore he is able to save completely those who come to God through him, because he always lives to intercede for them.

Hebrews 11:6 And without faith it is impossible to please God, because anyone who comes to him must believe that he exists and that he rewards those who earnestly seek him.

James 4:8 Come near to God and he will come near to you. Wash your hands, you sinners, and purify your hearts, you double-minded.

6. **Hebrews 11.6 is a pivotal verse on drawing near to God. What two things are required to draw near to God?**

The Bible is big on rewards. Hebrews 11.6 is one of my all-time favorite verses. It says we cannot come to God unless we believe that God exists and that He rewards those who earnestly seek Him. We cannot come to God unless we believe that God is a rewarder.

I don't think this is saying that God would prevent access if we don't believe some magical thing. It is just stating the nature of things. We will not pursue God unless we believe that God is a rewarder. We will not pursue God unless we believe that we will be rewarded. We naturally pursue what we believe to be is in our best interest. If we don't believe it is in our best interest to follow God, we won't follow God.

Jesus had a lot to say about this. In the Sermon on the Mount, Jesus warns us not to do our good works with the motive of wanting to be seen by men. He gives us this motivation: if we have the motivation of wanting to be seen by men, we will receive the reward of being seen by men. Jesus says to hold out for the big reward: the reward that will come from God. Jesus said to let your giving be done in secret and your Father will reward you. Hold out for that big reward. Don't settle for the little reward. Jesus taught that most of our prayer life should be private, and if we live that way, we will receive a greater reward.

This teaching is based on the foundation of the Old Testament teaching that often has the phrase, "That it may go well with you." We are told to obey the commands so that it will go well with us. Obedience always has its rewards. God is big into rewards. Here are a few examples. (Emphasis added.) — Josh Hunt, *Break a Habit; Make a Habit* (2020 Vision, 2013).

7. Why is it necessary that we believe God is a rewarder?

God is a rewarder. It is impossible for me to draw near to God except that I believe that God is a rewarder. If God is a rewarder, I will be rewarded for seeking Him. It is always in my best interest to live the Christian life. It is always good for me to follow God.

This is important because we are all irrevocably hardwired to do what we believe to be in our best interest. The key word is believe. This is why faith is so important to Christian living. What we believe determines what we do. If we believe that God is good; if we believe that He is smart; if we believe that He has our best interest at heart; then trusting Him is relatively easy.

But if in my heart of hearts I believe that God is not good, that He can't be trusted, that He is not after my well-being, it is impossible—impossible for me to draw near to Him. Not because this belief that God is a rewarder is some kind of magic key that opens the door; it is simply the nature of things. I am irrevocably hardwired to do what I believe to be is in my best interest. I will only seek God if I really believe He is a rewarder.

I must come to love the Christian life or I will never come to live the Christian life. The people you teach must come to love the Christian life or they will never come to live the Christian life.

Prayer must become for them a sweet hour of prayer, or I will bet they didn't pray this morning.

Service is either a joy or a struggle.

Self-control will only get us so far. We will only make it so far forcing ourselves to do what we fundamentally don't believe is in our best interest. Sooner or later we will do what we believe is best for us. We either come to believe that God is good, that God is a rewarder, that it is good for us to follow God, or we will not follow God very far.

There is a place in Christian living for self-control. There are times when we must force ourselves to do what we don't feel like doing in the moment. There are times we must force ourselves to give even when it hurts. But, we either become joyful givers or we end up becoming stingy, selfish, people.

We must come to love the Christian life, or we will never come to live the Christian life. This is the key to application.
— Josh Hunt, *The Effective Bible Teacher*, 2013.

8. What does James 4.8 teach us about drawing near to God?

Some of us have tried to have a daily quiet time and have not been successful. Others of us have a hard time concentrating. And all of us are busy. So rather than spend time with God, listening for his voice, we'll let others spend time with him and then benefit from their experience. Let them tell us what God is saying. After all, isn't that why we pay preachers? ...

If that is your approach, if your spiritual experiences are secondhand and not firsthand, I'd like to challenge you with this thought: Do you do that with others parts of your life? ...

You don't do that with vacations.... You don't do that with romance.... You don't let someone eat on your behalf, do you? [There are] certain things no one can do for you.

And one of those is spending time with God. — *Just Like Jesus* / Max Lucado and Terri A. Gibbs, *Grace for the Moment: Inspirational Thoughts for Each Day of the Year* (Nashville, TN: J. Countryman, 2000), 138.

9. Is drawing near to God easy or hard?

Jesus said his yoke is easy and his burden is light. (Matthew 11.30) I have asked this question to countless audiences: Is Christian living easy or hard. Always, always, always, the answer comes back as a chorus: HARD! Christians have found Jesus' yoke to be hard when he promised it would be easy.

My experience is that it is either easy or impossible. It is easy because it is not me living it. It is Christ living his life in me. "I no longer live, but Christ lives in me." (Galatians 2.20) It is easy because I realize that my self-interest aligns with God's interests for my life. God is a rewarder. I will be rewarded for following him. He is good. It is always good to follow Him. It is always good for me to live the Christian life. What could be easier than doing what is good for me?

I can testify that this is often (though not always) how I feel. You probably feel that way at times as well. The question is,

"Why don't we feel that way more than we do?" And, more importantly, "Is there one habit we can develop that will lead us to that life?" — Josh Hunt, *Break a Habit; Make a Habit* (2020 Vision, 2013).

10. Verse 3. What does he mean by calling the leaders roaring lions and evening wolves?

In these verses Judah's corrupt leaders are addressed. Her political leaders' oppressive behavior is compared to that of roaring lions and evening wolves who ferociously devoured their prey (cp. Mic. 3:9-10). According to Wright, "Zephaniah's use of 'evening wolves' (3:3; cp. Hab. 1:8) to describe Judah's judges was particularly sinister. Wolves habitually lay low throughout the day until dusk, striking when other animals are tired and ready to bed down for the night. They usually descend in packs, tearing their prey and gorging themselves on flesh. Jesus described false prophets as 'ravenous wolves' (Matt. 7:15 RSV), and the apostle Paul referred to false teachers as 'fierce wolves' not sparing the flock (Acts 20:29 RSV)" (Wright, 87).

Degradation among the people often reflects a failure of spiritual leadership. Not surprisingly, Zephaniah declared that apostasy among Judah's spiritual leaders was rampant. The word treacherous essentially denotes unfaithfulness in dealings with God or other people. These prophets were probably guilty of unfaithfulness in both areas. Priests were to teach the law (Ezra 7:12; 2 Chr. 15:3), but these had violated the law and profaned the sanctuary, evidently by their idolatry (Zeph. 1:4-5) and by offering blemished animals. — *Holman Old Testament Commentary – Nahum-Malachi.*

11. What do you learn about God from verse 8?

As we see in the history of Israel and in our own life, our long-suffering God is merciful and patient despite His people's continual rebellion. God's love for His people, however, compels Him to hate that which destroys us, so He abhors sin. The reality is that those who reject His love and cling to their sin must face His overwhelming wrath.

"All the earth shall be devoured with the fire of My jealousy," God proclaims through Zephaniah (3:8). God's purposes require Him to discipline and even judge His people. Are you willing to undergo the disciplinary pruning process until God has purged you of your sin?

Remember that the purpose of God's discipline is to purify you so you can enjoy fellowship with Him who loves you dearly. He longs to care for you and comfort you, and He rejoices when you seek Him.

One more thing. You are not one of faceless, nameless millions. He knows you personally. He loves you and celebrates your love for Him. His wrath is simply the response of His holiness to lethal sin that will destroy you. — Henry Blackaby and Richard Blackaby, *Discovering God's Daily Agenda* (Nashville: Thomas Nelson, 2007).

12. Verse 12 says that God won't destroy everyone. Who will He not destroy?

Something remaining. In the Old Testament some passages refer to total destruction of a nation (e.g., the Babylonians in Jer. 50:26). When God brings judgment on the people, however, he does not destroy the faithful with the wicked, but leaves a remnant (Ezek. 6:8; Mic. 2:12). The concept of a remnant stood for that part of the nation who were faithful even though most people rejected the ways of God (Isa. 4:2–4). The fact of the existence of a remnant is said to be due to God himself (Isa. 1:9; Zeph. 3:12). The remnant, then, is the real people of God, a concept we also find in the New Testament, "a remnant chosen by grace" (Rom. 11:5). — Galaxie Software, *10,000 Sermon Illustrations* (Biblical Studies Press, 2002).

13. What does it mean to be meek? What is the difference between meekness and humility?

In our culture, meekness has come to mean weakness. But that is not the biblical view. A wild horse which has been broken is no less strong, but he has been made useful to man.

Jesus was meek, but by no stretch of the imagination was He weak. Jesus was and is God.

What did He mean, then, when He said that the meek will inherit the earth? He was speaking of an attitude, a form of humility that is sorely lacking in our culture. A famous baseball coach once declared that "nice guys finish last." One of the best-selling books a few years ago was Looking Out for Number One. A recent decade was described by some sociologists as the "me decade."

No person is meek by nature. It is the work of the Spirit of God. Moses was meek, but he was not meek by nature. God worked meekness into him over a forty-year period. Peter was certainly not meek by nature. He was impetuous, saying and doing the first thing that came into his mind. The Holy Spirit of God transformed Peter after the resurrection of Jesus. Before his conversion, Paul was not meek. His job was to persecute Christians! Yet Paul wrote to the church at Galatia, "The fruit of the Spirit is . . . gentleness, goodness . . . meekness."

It is our human nature to be proud, not meek. Only the Spirit of God can transform our lives through the new birth experience and then make us over again into the image of Christ, our example of what pleases God in the way of meekness. — Billy Graham, *Unto the Hills: A Daily Devotional* (Nashville: Thomas Nelson, 2010).

14. Who is an example of meekness?

When you hear the word meekness you may think of the word in its modern setting—someone who is spineless, spiritless, lacking in strength and virility. The meek person in today's world is not how we'd like to be known. But the Bible says, "Blessed are the meek."

The Bible says the meek are blessed of God and someday they will rule the earth.

Meekness is not weakness. It is not laziness. It is not compromise at any price, not just being born nicer than other people.

The word came to mean in classical Greek "to soothe, to calm, to tranquilize." Someone has described meekness as gentleness by those who have the power to be otherwise—power under control. Meekness is the grace that brings strength and gentleness together.

When Jesus invited us to Him, He did not appeal to us on the basis of His kingship, majesty, or authority. The Lord reaches out His arms and says, "Come to Me and I'll give you rest, for I am meek—you can be comfortable coming to Me" (see Matthew 11:28). — David Jeremiah, *Sanctuary: Finding Moments of Refuge in the Presence of God* (Nashville, TN: Integrity Publishers, 2002), 153.

15. How do we become meek?

In our modern English idiom the word meek is hardly one of the honourable words of life. Nowadays it carries with it an idea of spinelessness, and subservience, and mean-spiritedness. It paints the picture of a submissive and ineffective creature. But it so happens that the word meek—in Greek praus (<G4239>)—was one of the great Greek ethical words.

Aristotle has a great deal to say about the quality of meekness (praotis = <G4236>). It was Aristotle's fixed method to define every virtue as the mean between two extremes. On the one hand there was the extreme of excess; on the other hand there was the extreme of defect; and in between there was the virtue itself, the happy medium. To take an example, on the one extreme there is the spendthrift; on the other extreme there is the miser; and in between there is the generous man.

Aristotle defines meekness, praotes (<G4236>), as the mean between orgilotes (see orge, <G3709>), which means excessive anger, and aorgesia, which means excessive angerlessness. Praotes (<G4236>), meekness, as Aristotle saw it, is the happy medium between too much and too little anger. — *Barclay's Daily Study Bible (NT).*

16. What good things come to the humble?

James's final command sums up all the others: "Humble yourselves in the sight of the Lord, and He will lift you up" (James 4:10). This is the humility of genuine repentance. How do we humble ourselves? Through all the means James has just listed: Submit to God, resist the devil, draw near to God, cleanse your hands, purify your hearts, lament, mourn, weep, and get into a serious frame of mind about your sin.

James preceded this list of ten imperatives by saying, "God resists the proud, but gives grace to the humble" (v. 6). He was quoting from the Greek translation of Proverbs 3:34: "Surely He scorns the scornful, but gives grace to the humble." — John F. MacArthur Jr., *Can God Bless America?: The Biblical Pathway to Blessing* (Nashville, TN: W Pub. Group, 2002), 26–27.

17. God loves the humble. Do you? Do you find humble people or proud people more likable?

Humility is attractive because it accepts others. You feel valued and important when you are in the presence of humility. Those who are humble are not pressing their agenda; rather, they are listening for your needs, dreams, and fears. Humility is other centric. It is also in position to trust God. You tend to trust those who trust God. They depend on their heavenly Father because they recognize their limitations without Him.

Humility also solicits followers. People want to follow a person of humility. They respect the honesty that travels with humility. This is vital to effective leadership. People will go the extra mile for an honest and humble leader. They serve with passion because they feel they are served and cared for by their humble leader. However, humility not only attracts positive reactions but negative ones as well. — Boyd Bailey, *Seeking Daily the Heart of God Volume Ii* (Atlanta: Wisdom Hunters, 2013).

18. What do we learn about God from Zephaniah 3.17? What do we learn about ourselves?

Let this truth sink in: God takes great delight in you. He rejoices over you with singing. We have songs we sing about God. Did you know He has love songs He sings about you? — Josh Hunt, *Enjoying God* (Josh Hunt, 2000).

19. Do you think of God as taking great delight in you?

Imagine! The God of the entire universe who created the stars with the command of his resonant voice rejoices over you with singing! The God of the entire universe loves you and takes delight in you. If that doesn't cause you to smile, you may want to check your pulse.

Do you see yourself as someone who is beloved by God? Better yet, do you feel that you are the apple of your Father's eye? Do the people you teach feel that they are God's beloved? If not, I invite you to pray right now and tell God you want to exchange whatever belief you have about yourself for the truth that you are the beloved of God. Then I would encourage you to lead your class to do the same. Until their self-image is one of being loved by God, they will never behave as children of God. — Josh Hunt, *Disciplemaking Teachers*, 1996.

20. What do you want to recall from today's conversation?

21. How can we support one another in prayer this week?

7 Minor Prophets, Lesson #4

Good Questions Have Small Groups Talking

www.joshhunt.com

Again, I'd email your group and ask them to do a little background reading. It is almost impossible to get fully up to speed on a passage like this with a little background reading. They don't need to do a lot of reading. Half an hour or so reading the notes in a study Bible will make the conversation a whole lot more interesting. Alternatively, you might email just a few of your readers and ask them to give a brief report on some of the background info.

Obadiah

OPEN

Let's each share your name and how many times have you been out of the country, if ever.

DIG

1. **Review. We have looked at two prophets so far. What do you recall about Nahum?**

   Long after Jonah had stirred Nineveh to repentance, Nahum foretold the mighty city's total destruction. He describes the cruelty of the Assyrians as they conquer nation after nation. He predicts the siege and destruction of the city and the end of the Assyrian empire. — *The New International Version* (Grand Rapids, MI: Zondervan, 2011), Na.

2. **What do you recall about Zephaniah?**

   Zephaniah focused on the coming "day of the Lord" that would purge Judah. He encourages the people to return to God before the day of judgment. He also predicted the judgment and destruction of neighboring nations, but ended with a note of hope—God would bring his people home and restore their honor among the nations. — *The New International Version* (Grand Rapids, MI: Zondervan, 2011), Zep.

3. **Before you read any of the prophets, it is nice to acquaint yourself with some background. A good study Bible is invaluable in this regard. What do we know about the background of Obadiah?**

   A struggle that began in the womb between twin brothers, Esau and Jacob, eventually erupted into a greater struggle between their respective descendants, the Edomites and the Israelites. The prophet Obadiah roundly condemned the Edomites for their stubborn refusal to aid Israel, first during the time of the wilderness wandering (Num. 20:14–21) and later during the time of the Babylonian invasion. This little-known prophet described their crimes, tried their case, and pronounced their judgment: total destruction. By contrast, God promised that his people would ultimately destroy their enemies and live in peace.

   Obadiah is the shortest book of the Old Testament and in it, Obadiah addresses Edom's prideful and superior attitude after the enemies of Israel had crushed her. He knew that a similar end would come to Edom, and that God would eventually restore Israel to her land and place of prominence.

The Hebrew name Obadyah means "Worshiper of Yahweh" or "Servant of Yahweh." Nothing more is known of the prophet other than what he reveals in the brief twenty-one verses of his prophecy.

Themes: God provides and cares for His people and will execute judgment against those who oppose them.

Author: Obadiah.

Time: Approximately 840 B.C.

Structure: Verses 1–16 of Obadiah foretell the destruction of Edom, while verses 17–21 speak of the deliverance of Zion. —Charles F. Stanley, *The Charles F. Stanley Life Principles Bible: New King James Version* (Nashville, TN: Nelson Bibles, 2005), Ob.

4. Obadiah 1.1 identifies this prophecy as a prophecy to Edom. Locate Edom on a map.

Map: ESV Study Bible.

5. Who were the Edomites? Where did they come from?

THE BOOK OF OBADIAH IS ONE OF ONLY TWO MINOR prophets that is addressed entirely to a nation other than Israel or Judah. It deals with the ancient feud between Israel and the nation of Edom, between the descendants of Jacob and those of his brother Esau. Through the prophet Obadiah, the Lord expressed His indignation at the nation of Edom. When they should have been helping their relatives, they were gloating over the Israelites' problems and raiding their homes. A day was coming—the day of the Lord—when all these wrongs would be righted. The Lord would bring justice to the world.

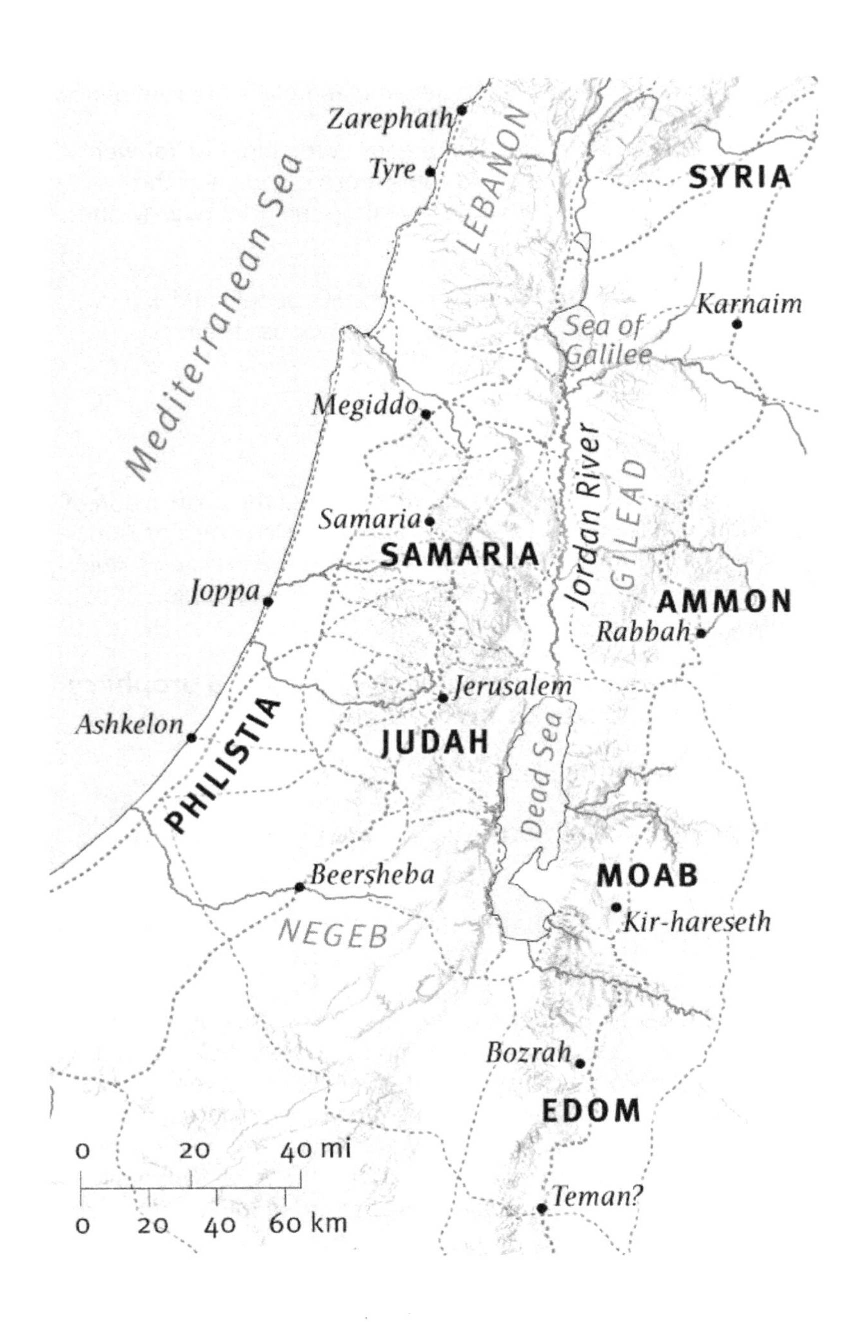
Zarephath
Tyre
LEBANON
SYRIA
Mediterranean Sea
Karnaim
Sea of Galilee
Megiddo
Jordan River
GILEAD
Samaria
SAMARIA
Joppa
AMMON
Rabbah
Jerusalem
Ashkelon
PHILISTIA
JUDAH
Dead Sea
MOAB
Beersheba
Kir-hareseth
NEGEB
Bozrah
EDOM
0
20
40 mi
0
20
40
60 km
Teman?

In 586 B.C. Nebuchadnezzar's army crushed Judah and destroyed Jerusalem and Solomon's temple, ending Judah's existence as an independent nation. Edom, as a closely related nation, should have helped Judah's refugees. But instead of offering sympathy and help, Edom handed Judeans over to the conquering Babylonians. The Edomites even murdered some of the refugees. Such treachery to a related nation could not be overlooked. God gave Obadiah a stern message for Edom, a warning of God's judgment on them for their callous treatment of the fleeing Judeans.

The Edomites' pride and presumed self-sufficiency became their downfall. Their fortress capital of Sela, which they considered impregnable, became their tomb. Their Arab neighbors turned on them, taking over their land and their livelihood. The Edomites were pushed into what had been southern Judah. In the second century B.C., the resurgent Jewish kingdom under the Maccabees conquered the Edomites and forcibly converted them to Judaism. At that time they were called Idumeans. — Earl D. Radmacher, Ronald Barclay Allen, and H. Wayne House, *Nelson's New Illustrated Bible Commentary* (Nashville: T. Nelson Publishers, 1999), Ob.

6. How do you imagine this history might have affected the relationship between Judah and Edom?

In the shortest book of the Old Testament, the prophet Obadiah warns the nation of Edom that their gloating over Israel's troubles must stop. Their mockery of God's chosen people is about to call down His wrath. Ironically, the fathers of each nation were brothers—Jacob, who birthed the Israelites, and Esau, who founded Edom.

This tiny book reminds us of the staying power of negativity. The international vendetta grew out of sibling rivalry, which began when Jacob deceptively stole Esau's birthright. Jacob attempted reconciliation many years later, but Esau's bitterness ran too deep. It lived on in his descendants, who gleefully watched their brothers suffer God's judgment.

Centuries after Jacob and Esau fought over their inheritance, Moses and Jacob's descendants faced continuing antagonism from Edom. Guiding his people through the desert, Moses requested safe passage through the country, but the Edomite king refused, threatening to attack (see Num. 20:14–21). Moses was forced to lead the Israelites around the country's perimeter.

I've long observed this law of "enduring negativity"—the uncanny tendency for jealousy, bitterness, and other kinds of negative bias to exhibit unusually long shelf lives. In The Subtlety of Emotions, the author writes, "People ruminate about events inducing strong negative emotions five times as long as they do about events inducing strong positive ones."57

Negativity's emotional power over us is immense. In The Science of Happiness, the authors write, "A melodrama will move us much more easily than a comedy. . . . If you show subjects in neuropsychological experiments happy and sad pictures, they will spontaneously respond more strongly to the latter."58 Another book, Sway: The Irresistible Pull of Irrational Behavior, corroborates: "We experience the pain associated with a loss much more vividly than we do the joy of experiencing a gain. . . . For no apparent logical reason, we overreact to perceived losses."59 — Tom R. Harper, *Leading from the Lion's Den* (Nashville: B&H, 2010).

7. One more background question. What is the date of Obadiah—give or take 100 years?

Radmacher, Earl D., Ronald Barclay Allen, and H. Wayne House. *Nelson's New Illustrated Bible Commentary.* Nashville: T. Nelson Publishers, 1999.

8. Verse 3. What was the main pride of Edom?

The pride of thine heart hath deceived thee, thou that dwellest in the clefts of the rock, whose habitation is high; that saith in his heart, Who shall bring me down to the ground?

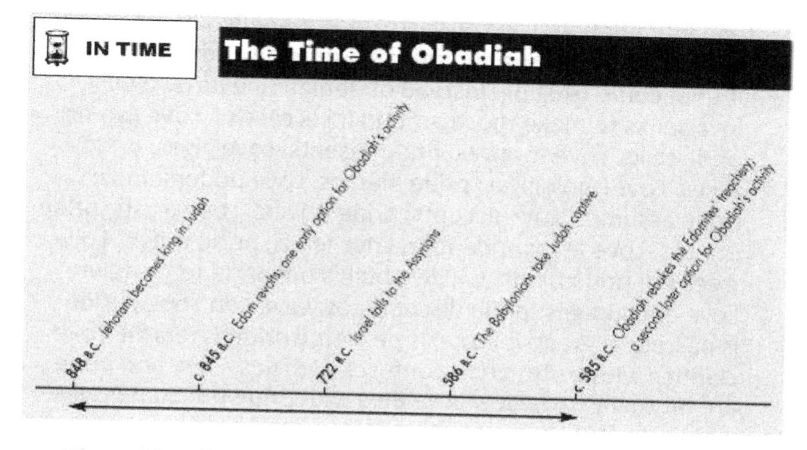

The pride of thy heart: the Edomites were, as most mountaineers are, a rough, hardy, and daring people; necessitated sometimes to extraordinary adventures, and many times succeeded in attempts which others would not venture upon; hence they did swell in pride and confidence, and their hearts were bigger than their achievements, and they proud above measure. Hath deceived thee; magnifying thy strength above what really it is. Thou, people of Edom, that dwellest in the clefts of the rock; houses, fortresses, towns, and cities, built upon inaccessible rocks, which neither could be undermined nor scaled. Or, dwellest in dark, deep, and unsearchable caves amidst the rocks. That saith in his heart; who think with themselves, and are upon report of an invasion ready to say, Who shall bring me down to the ground? it is not possible for armies to approach to us, nor bring their engines to shake or batter our walls. Who shall? i.e. none can. — Matthew Poole, *Annotations upon the Holy Bible, vol. 2* (New York: Robert Carter and Brothers, 1853), 922.

9. What exactly is pride?

Pride's feeling of superiority slices into the soul like a surgeon's scalpel. It inserts its influence deep and wide. You can be controlled and wired by pride and not even know it. Love longs to have the same status as power-hungry pride. Love seeks to defuse pride's time bomb of terror and intimidation. Love outlasts pride if applied humbly and heavily. Love drives pride from a controlling heart and frees it to become trusting. Instead of demanding its own way, love seeks to make those around it successful. Love listens; pride talks. Love forgives; pride resents. Love gives; pride takes. Love apologizes; pride blames. Love understands; pride assumes. Love accepts; pride rejects. Love trusts; pride doubts. Love asks; pride tells. Love leads; pride drives. Love frees up; pride binds up. Love builds up; pride tears down. Love encourages; pride discourages. Love confronts; pride is passive-aggressive. Love is peaceful; pride is fearful. Love clarifies with truth; pride confuses with lies. Love and pride are mutually exclusive. Love dies with pride but comes alive with humility.

Most important, humility is a hotbed of love. It has the opposite effect on love than does pride. Humility invites love to take up permanent residence in the human heart. Love covers a multitude of sins (1 Peter 4:8), and humility understands that love is reserved for everyone. Love forgives even the worst of sinners, as pride struggles in a life of bitterness and resentment, thinking somehow it is paying back the offender. This state of unresolved anger only eats up the one unable to love and forgive. Furthermore, humility positions you to love and be loved. Humility knows it needs help in the arena of receiving agape love. Your humble heart yearns for love from your Lord Jesus Christ. Once you receive the love of your heavenly Father, you can't help but dispense it to others hungry for a hug. As you receive love, you are capable of giving love. Therefore, let the Lord love on you and allow others to love you, so you can, in turn, love. Proud hearts melt under the influence of intense and unconditional love. The calling of Christians is perpetual love; so be guilty of love.

Your love is healing and inviting. Pride exits when humility enters, and then you are in a position to love. — Boyd Bailey, *Seeking Daily the Heart of God* (Atlanta: Wisdom Hunters, 2011).

10. What bad things come to the proud?

Love is not proud. Indeed, there is no room for pride in a heart of love. Pride is an anchor to love that restrains its rich offering. It prolongs the inability to love by short-circuiting the effect of agape love. Pride is a precursor to loveless living; it struggles with love because it requires a focus off itself and onto others. Pride is deceptive, as it always negotiates for its own benefit. There is a driving force behind pride that is unhealthy and unnecessary. Moreover, it is indiscriminate in its seduction of either gender. Men may be the most susceptible to pride's illusion, but women can be deceived just as well. Eve fell into this trap in her encounter with the devil (1 Timothy 2:14). — Boyd Bailey, *Seeking Daily the Heart of God* (Atlanta: Wisdom Hunters, 2011).

11. Do the proud know they are proud? If I am prideful, am I likely aware of it? Can you see pride in the mirror?

C. S. Lewis spoke of pride:

> In God you come up against something which is in every respect immeasurably superior to yourself. Unless you know God as that—and, therefore, know yourself as nothing in comparison—you do not know God at all. As long as you are proud you cannot know God. A proud man is always looking down on things and people and, of course, as long as you are looking down, you cannot see something that is above you.
>
> The virtue opposite to it, in Christian morals, is called humility ... The utmost evil is pride. Unchastity, anger, greed, drunkenness, and all that are mere fleabites in comparison. It was through pride that the devil became the devil. Pride leads to every other vice. It is the complete anti-God state of mind ...
>
> If you want to find out how proud you are, the easiest way is to ask yourself, "How much do I dislike it when other people snub me, or refuse to take any notice of me, or patronize me, or show off?... Is it because I wanted

> to be the big noise at the party that I am so annoyed at someone else being the big noise?" ... Pride gets no pleasure out of having something, only out of having more of it than the next man.

The greatest struggle of a believer is with pride. All other sins flow from this one polluted stream. Ask God to free you from pride's grasp. Boundless freedom awaits those who make the journey. — Charles F. Stanley, *Into His Presence* (Nashville, TN: Thomas Nelson Publishers, 2000), 29.

12. Verse 3. How did their geography contribute to their pride? If you have a smart phone, you might do a search for pictures of Edom.

This land of mountain peaks and narrow gorges, steep cliffs and deep chasms that form some of the wildest rock scenery in the world gave the Edomites a feeling of self-confidence and an air of invincibility. 'Who can bring [us] down to the ground?' was their boast. They imagined that no man, no army, no god could reach or overcome them. They did not doubt the safety of their lofty fortifications even when the armies of God were marshalling their forces against them. The pride of their hearts had deceived them (cf. Jeremiah 17:9). — Tim Shenton, *Nahum and Obadiah: An Expositional Commentary, Exploring the Bible Commentary* (Leominster, UK: Day One Publications, 2007), 86.

13. What are people in our world proud of today?

This is what the LORD says: "Let not the wise boast of their wisdom or the strong boast of their strength or the rich boast of their riches, but let the one who boasts boast about this: that they have the understanding to know me, that I am the LORD, who exercises kindness, justice and righteousness on earth, for in these I delight," declares the LORD. Jeremiah 9:23–24 (NIV)

14. What is God's solution to pride?

When we see ourselves as "pretty good," we misunderstand the gravity of sin and our desperate need for grace. We place

ourselves above others, become their judges, and give them the power to disappoint us.

A physicist friend uses this analogy: Each of us is like a lightbulb. One shines with fifty watts of holiness, another has only twenty-five watts. Maybe the most stellar Christians are two hundred watts. But these comparisons become trite in the presence of the sun.

In the face of God, our different levels of piety are puny and meaningless. It makes no sense to compare ourselves with one another, because we are all much more alike than we are different. —Mark McMinn, Why Sin Matters (Tyndale, 2004) / Craig Brian Larson and Phyllis Ten Elshof, 1001 *Illustrations That Connect* (Grand Rapids, MI: Zondervan Publishing House, 2008), 337.

15. Verses 5, 6. Anyone have a study Bible with a note on this verse? How as this prophecy fulfilled?

Because Edom was thought to be impregnable, banks carved in the cliffs of the rock city of Petra were devoted to holding the treasures of her allies. Here, the Lord says,

"Every last one of your treasures will be stolen." When Petra was rediscovered in the early 1800s, although the buildings that were carved right out of rock were still intact, not a single item was found within them. Considering Petra had a population of one million, the fact that there wasn't a single artifact left not only fulfills Obadiah's prophecy, but makes it unique in the history of archeology. — Jon Courson, *Jon Courson's Application Commentary: Volume Two: Psalms-Malachi* (Nashville, TN: Thomas Nelson, 2006), 806.

16. Verse 12, 13. What is the application to our lives from these verses?

When you win a major bid or take a customer away from a competitor, enjoy the victory but don't gloat. Gloating leads only to overconfidence and may well kindle anger and retaliation from your competitor.

In the past, one particular rival repeatedly gloated over taking a large account away from my firm. After a while, I established a designated file with the names of all my competitors' accounts, which I then made a special project of working to obtain. As a direct result of their smug attitude, I worked their prospects harder.

When you do land a big account, recognize that your work is just beginning. Instead of gloating, focus your enthusiasm and energy on serving your new customer and obtaining the next one. — Steve Marr, *Proverbs for Business* (Grand Rapids, MI: Revell, 2006).

17. Does your translation have anything other than gloat?

NCV | Ob 12 Edom, do not **laugh at** your brother Israel in his time of trouble or be happy about the people of Judah when they are destroyed. Do not brag when cruel things are done to them.

NIV84 | Ob 12 You should not **look down** on your brother in the day of his misfortune, nor rejoice over the people of

Judah in the day of their destruction, nor boast so much in the day of their trouble.

CEV | Ob 12 Why did you **celebrate** when such a dreadful disaster struck your relatives? Why were you so pleased when everyone in Judah was suffering?

KJV 1900 | Ob 12 But thou shouldest not have **looked on** the day of thy brother in the day that he became a stranger; Neither shouldest thou have rejoiced over the children of Judah in the day of their destruction; Neither shouldest thou have spoken proudly in the day of distress.

NKJV | Ob 12 "But you should not have **gazed on** the day of your brother In the day of his captivity; Nor should you have rejoiced over the children of Judah In the day of their destruction; Nor should you have spoken proudly In the day of distress.

18. Proverbs 24.17. Someone read that for us. What does it mean to gloat? Why is it bad to gloat?

What does it mean to gloat? The dictionary says it means to "gaze in malicious pleasure" at someone else's misfortune. Sounds pretty coldhearted, doesn't it? It takes a low character to find pleasure in someone else's pain. But what if the hurting person had it coming? What if he's been a source of pain and grief in your life? What if he deliberately set out to hurt you, and it backfired? Isn't it natural to find just a little satisfaction when your enemies are getting what they deserve?

Jesus set the standard for the way we should treat those who hurt us, and it doesn't involve gloating. Jesus knew that God would see that justice was done, so we don't have to. Therefore, Jesus commands us to respond with love, prayer, and forgiveness to those who hurt us (Matthew 5:43–45). A hard-hearted response toward our enemy reveals that we, too, have evil in our hearts. It shows that we are no better than the person who injured us. Today's proverb warns that our sinful response when another person is under God's discipline may cause God to release our enemy and turn his discipline on us.

If you find yourself taking pleasure in someone else's pain, recognize that you are sinning. Hurry to seek God's forgiveness, and ask him to help you see your enemy through Christ's loving eyes. When you see someone as God does, you won't feel like gloating. — Henry Blackaby and Richard Blackaby, *The Experience* (Nashville: B&H, 1999).

19. What bad things come to those who gloat?

A big city lawyer was called in on a case between a farmer and a large railroad company. A farmer noticed that his prize cow was missing from the field through which the railroad passed. He filed suit against the railroad company for the value of the cow. The case was to be tried before the justice of the peace in the back room of the general store. The attorney immediately cornered the farmer and tried to get him to settle out of court. The lawyer did his best selling job, and the farmer finally agreed to take half of what he was claiming to settle the case. After the farmer signed the release and took the check, the young lawyer couldn't help but gloat a little over his success. He said to the farmer, "You know, I hate to tell you this but I put one over on you in there. I couldn't have won the case. The engineer was asleep and the fireman was in the caboose when the train went through your farm that morning. I didn't have one witness to put on the stand." The old farmer replied, "Well, I'll tell you, young feller, I was a little worried about winning that case myself because that durned cow came home this morning!" — Lowell D. Streiker, *Nelson's Big Book of Laughter: Thousands of Smiles from A to Z, electronic ed.* (Nashville: Thomas Nelson Publishers, 2000), 110.

20. How are gloating and pride related?

This is both the first term to be used and the only one which occurs twice. It is translated in various ways including 'gloat over', 'look down upon', 'gazed on', and 'looked on'. But although the term is very simple, it is a certain sort of looking which is condemned here and, from the way in which verse 12 develops, it is clear what sort of looking it was. The Edomites looked on at the 'day' of their brother and at his 'disaster' with something between indifference and pleasure: indifference, in the sense of caring not at all about Judah's suffering; pleasure, in the sense that there was malice, hatred, spite, vengefulness and the desire to benefit from the disaster (see also Ps. 22:17; 118:7; Micah 7:8). Matthew Henry comments, 'We must take heed with what eye we look upon the afflictions of our brethren; and, if we cannot look upon them with a gracious eye of sympathy and tenderness, it is better not to look upon them at all.' — David Field, *Obadiah: A Practical Commentary, Exploring the Bible Commentary* (Leominster: Day One Publications, 2008), 58.

21. What do you want to recall from today's conversation?

22. How can we support one another in prayer this week?

7 Minor Prophets, Lesson #5

Good Questions Have Small Groups Talking

www.joshhunt.com

Again, I'd email your group and ask them to do a little background reading. It is almost impossible to get fully up to speed on a passage like this with a little background reading. They don't need to do a lot of reading. Half an hour or so reading the notes in a study Bible will make the conversation a whole lot more interesting. Alternatively, you might email just a few of your readers and ask them to give a brief report on some of the background info.

Zechariah 8, 9

OPEN

Let's each share your name and one thing you are grateful for.

DIG

1. **Look at your Bible's Table of Contents. What do you recall about any of the Minor Prophets?**

   The key to long term memory is review.

2. **Let me assign each of you one of the Minor Prophets. See if your Bible has anything to say about an approximate date. Let's see if we can put them in chronological order.**

   I think you will find that the order in the Bible is approximate chronological order.

3. **We always start with background and context. What is the background and context for Zechariah?**

   For a dozen years or more, the task of rebuilding the temple has been half completed. Zechariah is commissioned by God to encourage the people in their unfinished responsibility. Rather than exhorting them to action with strong words of rebuke, Zechariah seeks to encourage them to action by reminding them of the future importance of the temple. The temple must be built, for one day the Messiah's glory will inhabit it. But future blessing is contingent upon present obedience. The people are not merely building a building; they are building the future. With that as their motivation, they can enter into the building project with wholehearted zeal, for their Messiah is coming.

   Zekar-yah means "Yahweh Remembers" or "Yahweh Has Remembered." This theme dominates the whole book: Israel will be blessed because Yahweh remembers the covenant He made with the fathers. The Greek and Latin version of his name is Zacharias. — *The Open Bible: New King James Version, electronic ed.* (Nashville: Thomas Nelson Publishers, 1998).

4. **What year is this written—give or take 100 years?**

   The prophecies of the first eight chapters of Zechariah are explicitly dated between 520 B.C. and 518 B.C. Chapters 9–14 are undated but are most likely from the period about 516–500 B.C. when the Persian Empire was beginning to fall. — Thomas Nelson, *The Woman's Study Bible* (Nashville: Thomas Nelson, 1995).

5. What is the theme of Zechariah?

For a dozen or more years the Jewish community had not completed the temple. Rather than rebuking them, Zechariah encouraged them to action by reminding them of the future importance of the temple. He indicated that the temple must be built because Messiah's glory would one day fill the temple. He indicated that future blessing was contingent upon their present obedience. — Elmer Towns, *Bible Answers for Almost All Your Questions* (Nashville: Thomas Nelson, 2003).

6. How would you describe the tone of Zechariah 8?

Zechariah is a man intoxicated with the vision of the coming Kingdom. He therefore quickly leaves behind the ethical exhortations of 7:1–14 to rhapsodize once more over what God is going to do for his people. If Israel can be made to see what Zechariah has seen in his visions, then they will respond with that obedient love appropriate to life under God's rule. — Elizabeth Rice Achtemeier, *Nahum–Malachi, Interpretation, a Bible Commentary for Teaching and Preaching* (Atlanta, GA: John Knox Press, 1986), 136.

7. What does God reveal about Himself in this chapter?

When Zechariah reminded people of God's judgment in permitting the destruction of Jerusalem and the captivity of the surviving Israelites, they might well have wondered if God's affections had been transferred elsewhere. Quite to the contrary, chapter 8 begins with a statement of fervent love: "Thus says the LORD of hosts: I am jealous for Zion with great jealousy, and I am jealous for her with great wrath" (Zech. 8:2). This jealousy is a zealous ardor which God has for his people. It is because of this love that God returns with the promises that follow. — Richard D. Phillips, *Zechariah, ed. Richard D. Phillips, Philip Graham Ryken, and Iain M. Duguid, Reformed Expository Commentary* (Phillipsburg, NJ: P&R Publishing, 2007), 168.

8. **How is the Kingdom of God described in this passage?**

Much in this series of brief salvation oracles has already been said, but there are also some new announcements. First, Zechariah proclaims what life will be like in the coming Kingdom and what we need do to enter into it, and the picture he presents is one of the most profound and poetic to be found in the Old Testament. The Kingdom of God, says verses 4–5, will be like a public park, where the elderly can sit together and talk and bask in the sun, and little children can play in contentment and safety with nothing to threaten them—no pervert lurking in the shadows to lure one of them away with candy; no drug dealer waiting to peddle his poison to innocents; no child bruised or warped by abusive parents or stunted by poor nutrition or inadequate education; not even a bully among the group to terrorize the younger and weaker.

Children peacefully at play in a park—of such is the Kingdom of God! The picture explodes all our mythology and otherworldly misconceptions of the Kingdom as an ethereal never-never land, divorced from earthy realities. This is a picture of this world made new by the coming of God—its goodness confirmed and restored to that wholeness that its Creator intended for it from the beginning (cf. Gen. 1:31).

The Bible, throughout, pictures that goodness for us in terms of a little child: "Let the children come to me, and do not hinder them," Jesus said, "for to such belongs the kingdom of heaven" (Matt. 19:14). The Kingdom a playground for children!—and unless we turn and become like children in our humility, we will never enter into it (Matt. 18:3–4). There the child "shall play over the hole of the asp, and the weaned child shall put his hand on the adder's den" (Isa. 11:8)—the serpent of our sinfulness (Gen. 3:15) turned to harmlessness and a plaything for children! — Elizabeth Rice Achtemeier, *Nahum–Malachi, Interpretation, a Bible Commentary for Teaching and Preaching* (Atlanta, GA: John Knox Press, 1986), 136–137.

9. Verse 4 speaks of old men sitting in the streets. What is he getting at with this picture?

Due to His sovereignty rather than the people's religiosity, the Lord declares that Jerusalem would one day be known as a city of truth and holiness, a place where even old men would be able to walk the streets in safety. — Jon Courson, *Jon Courson's Application Commentary: Volume Two: Psalms-Malachi* (Nashville, TN: Thomas Nelson, 2006), 900.

10. Verse 5 speaks of children playing in the streets. What is that about?

The little child leads us (Isa. 11:6) in the Bible's conceptions of God's future; and when we think to join cause with God's purpose for his earth, we need ask ourselves if we are constructing a place where little children may play. Perhaps Prime Minister Golda Meier fleetingly caught that vision when she welcomed Anwar Sadat of Egypt on his historic peace-mission to Israel, not with the silver bowl or other art object so often exchanged between heads of state but with a simple present for his grandchildren.

God's Kingdom will not have come on this earth until its streets are fit for its children. But by the same token, it will not have come until its children are fit for its streets. Zechariah has given us a standard here for all our planned utopias, and set up against a little child, none of them measures up. But there came a child—there came God's child—who was fit for the Kingdom. And because he came, God's playground for all children surely comes. — Elizabeth Rice Achtemeier, *Nahum–Malachi, Interpretation, a Bible Commentary for Teaching and Preaching* (Atlanta, GA: John Knox Press, 1986), 137.

11. Verse 13. How are God's people described? Is it true of us?

How awesome to think that God has made you a blessing. Because you are a boon to others, He doesn't want you to be afraid of anything. Instead, God wants you to look around you. Take in everything and everyone. Where, amid all the ups and downs of this world, can you be a blessing to someone else, with or without her knowledge? Whose day can you make today? Whether it be through making food, donating money, or helping to rebuild someone's home, step out into the world. Be God's blessing. Sow your love and compassion, and reap an awesome harvest. — Compiled By Barbour Staff, *Quiet Moments for Busy Days: Encouraging Thoughts for Women* (Uhrichsville, OH: Barbour, 2014).

12. Can you think of other passages that speak to this theme—that we are blessed to be a blessing?

Why did God call Abraham? Why did He call me? Why did He call you?

Abraham was blessed to be blessing:

> All peoples on earth will be blessed through you."
> Genesis 12:3 (NIV)

Only those with money can help those without. Only those with strength can help the weak. Only those who are healthy can help the sick.

You are blessed to be a blessing. God wants to bless your socks of. He wants to bless your socks off so that you can bless the socks off of others. You are not to be the end of the line. You are to be the Jordan River, not the Dead Sea.

God brought Joseph to a place of position and prominence. Why? So that he could be a blessing to others.

Why do you think God gave you all the stuff that He has given you? Did you know that much of the world lives on a dollar or two a day?

Why do think God saved you, forgave you, gave you His Holy Spirit, gave you, and gave you spiritual blessings?

Do you think it selfish of you to go hard after the blessed life? It is not if your motive is right. You are blessed to be a blessing. — Josh Hunt, *Following God* (Pulpit Press, 2014).

13. Zechariah 9.9 – 12 predicts when King Jesus would walk into Jerusalem. How as He different from other kings? How was He different from what they expected?

At the age of thirty-three, Alexander rode upon his mighty steed, Bucephalus, surrounded by soldiers whose shields were shining, whose spears were glistening. Yet Zion's King, also thirty-three, came riding on a donkey. Why did Jesus ride on a donkey? Why didn't He come with an impressive display of might? Because in so doing, He is humble, touchable, relatable. In fact, so seemingly ordinary was Jesus that, even though He had been in the public eye for thirty-three years, the soldiers evidently needed Judas to identify Him (Mark 14:44). — Jon Courson, *Jon Courson's Application Commentary: Volume Two: Psalms-Malachi* (Nashville, TN: Thomas Nelson, 2006), 902.

14. Verse 9. The NIV describes Jesus as "righteous and victorious." How does your translation have it?

NIV | Zec 9:9 Rejoice greatly, Daughter Zion! Shout, Daughter Jerusalem! See, your king comes to you, righteous and victorious, lowly and riding on a donkey, on a colt, the foal of a donkey.

The Message | Zec 9:9 "Shout and cheer, Daughter Zion! Raise the roof, Daughter Jerusalem! Your king is coming! a good king who makes all things right, a humble king riding a donkey, a mere colt of a donkey.

NASB95 | Zec 9:9 Rejoice greatly, O daughter of Zion! Shout in triumph, O daughter of Jerusalem! Behold, your king is coming to you; He is just and endowed with salvation, Humble, and mounted on a donkey, Even on a colt, the foal of a donkey.

ESV | Zec 9:9 Rejoice greatly, O daughter of Zion! Shout aloud, O daughter of Jerusalem! Behold, your king is coming to you; righteous and having salvation is he, humble and mounted on a donkey, on a colt, the foal of a donkey.

NCV | Zec 9:9 Rejoice greatly, people of Jerusalem! Shout for joy, people of Jerusalem! Your king is coming to you. He does what is right, and he saves. He is gentle and riding on a donkey, on the colt of a donkey.

NIV84 | Zec 9:9 Rejoice greatly, O Daughter of Zion! Shout, Daughter of Jerusalem! See, your king comes to you, righteous and having salvation, gentle and riding on a donkey, on a colt, the foal of a donkey.

GNB | Zec 9:9 Rejoice, rejoice, people of Zion! Shout for joy, you people of Jerusalem! Look, your king is coming to you! He comes triumphant and victorious, but humble and riding on a donkey—on a colt, the foal of a donkey.

CEV | Zec 9:9 Everyone in Jerusalem, celebrate and shout! Your king has won a victory, and he is coming to you. He is humble and rides on a donkey; he comes on the colt of a donkey.

NKJV | Zec 9:9 "Rejoice greatly, O daughter of Zion! Shout, O daughter of Jerusalem! Behold, your King is coming to you; He is just and having salvation, Lowly and riding on a donkey, A colt, the foal of a donkey.

15. What do we learn about Jesus from this verse?

Zechariah here fleshes out the picture of the coming Branch who was promised in I Zechariah 3:8; 6:12. The Revised Standard Version has translated the two adjectives of verse 9d with "triumphant" and "victorious," to connote the coming king's victory in war, but probably neither is a proper rendering of the text. The Messiah is first of all "righteous," which means that he rules as a king should rule over his subjects. "Righteousness" is throughout the Bible the fulfillment of the demands of a relationship. Thus, the coming king will properly fulfill his role as king of his people and as judge over all the earth (cf. Jer. 23:5–6; Isa. 32:1).

> He shall not judge by what his eyes see,
> or decide by what his ears hear;
> but with righteousness he shall judge the poor,

> and decide with equity for the meek of the earth; ... (Isa. 11:3b–4a).

He will protect the weak and prosper the good and be like "the shadow of a mighty rock within a weary land" (Isa. 32:2). But he will do such things because he will be enabled to do them by God. In every one of these passages in the Old Testament dealing with the "righteousness" of the Messiah, he has that character as a gift from God (cf. also Ps. 72:1).

Similarly, the Davidic Messiah will be "saved" or "delivered" from his enemies by God; but once again, there is no hint of victory in war here (cf. Ps. 33:16), and it may be that the thought is more of "vindication"—of being "declared right," like the Suffering Servant in Second Isaiah (Isa. 49:4; 50:8–9; cf. 53:11–12). The Messiah's manner and cause are now those that have God's approval, and therefore his realm is one that will endure. — Elizabeth Rice Achtemeier, *Nahum–Malachi, Interpretation, a Bible Commentary for Teaching and Preaching* (Atlanta, GA: John Knox Press, 1986), 151.

16. Why do you think Jesus entered Jerusalem on a donkey?

Can't you hear the Roman soldiers garrisoned in Jerusalem snickering as they saw Jesus ride in on a donkey? When a Roman leader came cruising into a city, it wasn't on a donkey. No, Roman rulers rode black stallions followed by chariots and thousands of soldiers marching in step with shields gleaming. But I wonder what the Romans of this world will say when Jesus comes again, for next time He comes, it won't be on a donkey. He'll come back riding a white horse followed by ten thousands of His saints (Jude 14). You see, the first time Jesus came, He came as the suffering Servant. But the next time He comes, it will be as the conquering King. — Jon Courson, *Jon Courson's Application Commentary* (Nashville, TN: Thomas Nelson, 2003), 155.

17. What do we learn from this picture of Jesus about what it means to be Christlike?

In Matthew 11:29, Jesus says, "Take My yoke upon you and learn from Me, for I am gentle and lowly in heart, and you will find rest for your souls." Matthew 21:5 describes Jesus riding on the donkey in His triumphal entry into the city—a quotation of Zechariah. If there was ever a perfect picture of meekness, there it is. The King of Glory and Power, riding on a donkey, under control.

Paul wrote, "Now I, Paul, myself am pleading with you by the meekness and gentleness of Christ—who in presence am lowly among you, but being absent am bold toward you" (2 Corinthians 10:1). Jesus is the perfect example of meekness, for His power was always under control.

One of my pet peeves as a minister of the gospel is the pictures that paint Jesus as weak. Jesus was no weakling. He was a strong, virile, powerful man. In fact, the Holy Scriptures preserve for us at least three occasions when the anger of our Lord is described. I can talk about the compassion of Jesus—it's everywhere. But I want to discuss for a few minutes the times when Jesus was angry. The Bible says it's possible to be angry and not sin. Anger is only a sin when it is done for the wrong reason in the wrong way. — David Jeremiah, *Fruit of the Spirit: Study Guide* (Nashville, TN: Thomas Nelson Publishers, 1995), 91.

18. Was Jesus always gentle? Should we always be gentle?

In our modern English idiom the word meek is hardly one of the honourable words of life. Nowadays it carries with it an idea of spinelessness, and subservience, and mean-spiritedness. It paints the picture of a submissive and ineffective creature. But it so happens that the word meek—in Greek praus (<G4239>)—was one of the great Greek ethical words.

Aristotle has a great deal to say about the quality of meekness (praotis = <G4236>). It was Aristotle's fixed method to define every virtue as the mean between two extremes. On the one hand there was the extreme of excess; on the other hand there was the extreme of defect; and in between there was the virtue itself, the happy medium. To take an example, on the one extreme there is the spendthrift; on the other extreme there is the miser; and in between there is the generous man.

Aristotle defines meekness, praotes (<G4236>), as the mean between orgilotes (see orge, <G3709>), which means excessive anger, and aorgesia, which means excessive angerlessness. Praotes (<G4236>), meekness, as Aristotle saw it, is the happy medium between too much and too little anger. And so the first possible translation of this beatitude is:

Blessed is the man who is always angry at the right time, and never angry at the wrong time.

If we ask what the right time and the wrong time are, we may say as a general rule for life that it is never right to be angry for any insult or injury done to ourselves; that is something that no Christian must ever resent; but that it is often right to be angry at injuries done to other people. Selfish anger is always a sin; selfless anger can be one of the great moral dynamics of the world.

But the word praus (<G4239>) has a second standard Greek usage. It is the regular word for an animal which has been domesticated, which has been trained to obey the word of command, which has learned to answer to the reins. It is the word for an animal which has learned to accept control. — *Barclay's Daily Study Bible (NT).*

19. As we seek to follow Christ… when are we to be gentle, and when are we to turn over tables?

We will meditate together on what the Bible teaches about serving and about confronting when you need to confront. As we will see, getting along is not just being nice all the time. Sometimes, we need to turn over some tables. — Josh Hunt, *How to Get Along With Almost Anyone*, 2014.

20. What do you want to recall from today's conversation?

21. How can we support one another in prayer this week?

7 Minor Prophets, Lesson #6

Good Questions Have Small Groups Talking

www.joshhunt.com

Again, I'd email your group and ask them to do a little background reading. It is almost impossible to get fully up to speed on a passage like this with a little background reading. They don't need to do a lot of reading. Half an hour or so reading the notes in a study Bible will make the conversation a whole lot more interesting. Alternatively, you might email just a few of your readers and ask them to give a brief report on some of the background info.

Zechariah 13

OPEN

Let's each share your name and when is the last time you saw a fountain.

DIG

1. **Look at your Bible's Table of Contents. What do you recall about any of the Minor Prophets?**

   The key to long term memory is review.

2. **Let's review . . . which of these came first?**

   David or Daniel?

   Abraham or Adam?

   Joshua or Joseph?

   Isaac or Isaiah?

   Come up with your own pair, and the rest will put them in order.

3. **Zechariah 13.1 reminds me of an old hymn: There is a fountain. What is the fountain in this verse?**

   The fountain that would cleanse Israel from her sin began flowing when a soldier thrust a spear into Jesus' side as He hung on the Cross of Calvary. — Jon Courson, *Jon Courson's Application Commentary: Volume Two: Psalms-Malachi* (Nashville, TN: Thomas Nelson, 2006), 908.

4. **When we think of a fountain, we think of a spray of water at a park. How would they have thought about a fountain? What did a fountain do? What is the lesson?**

   This is a remarkable promise, because from this fountain comes a cleansing for "sin and uncleanness." It is therefore a particularly apt depiction of Jesus Christ's cleansing blood, shed upon the cross. This cleansing, the prophet says, will be made available to the house of David and the inhabitants of Jerusalem. Given the earlier statement that God's Spirit will make us mourn for the pierced one (Zech. 12:10), it is clearly the blood of the Messiah that comes forth to cleanse. — Richard D. Phillips, Zechariah, ed. Richard D. Phillips, Philip Graham Ryken, and Iain M. Duguid, *Reformed Expository Commentary* (Phillipsburg, NJ: P&R Publishing, 2007), 281.

5. **Repeat after me: I am cleansed of all my sin. Is that how you see yourself?**

Here is the really amazing truth that I learned from my own freedom experience. I read in 1 John 1:9 that if I am willing to confess my sins, God will forgive me and cleanse me from all of my unrighteousness. The key here is that it is God who cleanses me. I can't do it myself. When I admit that my actions, words, or thoughts are not pleasing to my God, he is willing and able to cleanse me of all unrighteousness. That still amazes me. When I admitted my lust and the hedonism in my heart that spawned it, God began healing and cleaning me. — Gary Smalley, *Change Your Heart, Change Your Life: How Changing What You Believe Will Give You the Great Life You've Always Wanted* (Nashville: Thomas Nelson, 2008).

6. **What does it feel like to be cleansed?**

This is what we have in the cleansing blood of Christ—propitiation toward God so that his wrath against sin is satisfied, and expiation toward us so that sin's defilement is removed.

What a difference this makes to the mournful soul! Here is a message for us to preach to our forlorn hearts, that God has opened a fountain to cleanse us from the penalty and defilement of our sin. Here is good news for those cast down by a sense of guilt and unworthiness—a fountain flowing forth from the wounds of Jesus Christ. John wrote about this in his first epistle, saying, "This is how we set our hearts at rest in his presence whenever our hearts condemn us. For God is greater than our hearts, and he knows everything" (1 John 3:19–20 NIV). When our downcast souls speak to us of misery and dread, this is God's own testimony that is greater, the testimony of a Savior who died in our place to reconcile us to God's love. In 1 John 1:9 we read, "If we confess our sins, he is faithful and just to forgive us our sins and to cleanse us from all unrighteousness."

This is wonderfully dramatized in John Bunyan's Pilgrim's Progress. The pilgrim, named Christian, had fled the coming wrath of God, seeking safety in the Celestial City. But his progress was hindered by a burden on his back, representing the weight of sin upon our souls. On the way he was met by Mr. Worldly Wiseman, who gave him worldly counsel on the removal of this burden of guilt, advising Christian to indulge himself in worldly comforts, adding a strong dose of morality, so that he could simply forget the burden. Christian found, however, that neither the pleasures of the world nor the pursuit of moral virtue removed the burden of this guilt of sin. On he journeyed, wearied by his load. Finally, Bunyan writes,

> He ran until he came to a peak where a cross stood; a little below, in the bottom was a tomb. When Christian reached the cross, his burden became loose, fell from his back, and tumbled into the tomb. I never saw the burden again.... As he stood looking and weeping, three Shining Ones approached and greeted him. "Peace," the first said, "Your sins are forgiven." The second removed his filthy rags and dressed him in rich clothing. The third put a mark on his forehead and gave him a sealed roll. He told Christian ... to leave it at the celestial gate [to enter the Celestial City].

Christ's cleansing fountain is given to speak peace and joy to mournful hearts. But we must believe this good news to have our burden relieved. Lloyd-Jones comments, "If you do not believe that word, and if you go on dwelling on your sin, I say that you are not accepting the Word of God, you are not taking God at His word, you do not believe what He tells you and that is your real sin." — Richard D. Phillips, Zechariah, ed. Richard D. Phillips, Philip Graham Ryken, and Iain M. Duguid, *Reformed Expository Commentary* (Phillipsburg, NJ: P&R Publishing, 2007), 284–285.

7. What are we to do if we don't feel forgiven of all of our sins?

Did you know that learning to forgive yourself is just as important as forgiving others? It's true, although it is an aspect of forgiveness that is overlooked frequently. When you forgive yourself—that is, you stop allowing guilt to tear you apart—you are letting God heal the brokenness hidden deep within.

Refusing to "let yourself off the hook" nurtures guilt. Along with guilt come shame, feelings of worthlessness, and a desire to hide from God. You may even harbor the subconscious idea that being free from guilt would foster a carefree attitude, which might steer you back into the same sin.

There is hope for you today. God desires for you to live in the freedom, security, and holiness that are yours in Christ. Through the Savior who paid for your sin, you are truly righteous and blameless. Romans 8:1 gives you this promise: "There is therefore now no condemnation to those who are in Christ Jesus."

If your self-image is blurred because you don't feel forgiven, embrace this promise as well: "If we confess our sins, He is faithful and righteous to forgive us our sins and to cleanse us from all unrighteousness" (1 John 1:9 NASB).

As you learn to forgive yourself as Christ forgives you, you may need to reaffirm these truths periodically. Remember, Christ came to set the captives free (Isa. 61:1). — Charles F. Stanley, *Seeking His Face* (Nashville, TN: Thomas Nelson Publishers, 2002), 69.

8. Verses 2 – 6. What happens after cleansing?

Changes have to be made when people are cleansed from their sin and impurity. God declares, 'Once you have been justified (made righteous), you need to be sanctified (the process of being made holy).' This is a lifelong procedure. God's people are required to live holy lives and they should strive after a life given over entirely to God and obedience to his commands. The message here is the same as that which has been spoken over and over again to the Jews. God's people are required to turn their backs upon their old lives and to start anew.

There were two major evils in the land—idolatry and false prophets. — Michael Bentley, *Building for God's Glory: Haggai and Zechariah Simply Explained, Welwyn Commentary Series* (Darlington, England: Evangelical Press, 1989), 209.

9. What does it mean that their sins will be remembered no more?

The purification of the land will cleanse it of every possible appearance of evil. Of the many that might be mentioned, however, Zechariah singles out only two evils that plagued the nation before the fall of the northern kingdom to Assyria in 721 B.C. and the fall of the southern kingdom to Babylon in 586 B.C.: idolatry and false prophecy.

These went together. In the age of Ahab and Jehoshaphat, when Micaiah was called to prophesy the death of Ahab by Ramoth Gilead, there were 400 false prophets but only one prophet of the Lord (1 Kings 22). Moreover, when Elijah appeared on Mount Carmel, there were 450 prophets of Baal but only one Elijah (1 Kings 18). Later, in the southern kingdom, Jeremiah was plagued by the many false prophets who predicted peace for Jerusalem when actually destruction was coming (Jer. 6:13-14; 8:10-11). When times were bad, idolatry and false prophecy went together and were widespread. In the prophesied day of genuine national repentance, both will be put away.

Zechariah makes three points about this time of purification. First, the idols will be so thoroughly removed that even the memory of them will be forgotten. That is a great promise, for anyone who has ever wrestled with sin knows that the memory of sin (accompanied by a persistent desire for it) often continues long after the sin itself has been repudiated. We remember Augustine's description of trying to free himself of sexual sins but finding even in his seclusion that his mind was thinking about the dancing girls in Rome. Sin lingers in the mind. But in this day, even the memory of idols will be taken away from God's people. — *Boice Expositional Commentary - An Expositional Commentary – The Minor Prophets, Volume 2: Micah-Malachi.*

10. This section speaks of idolatry. It reminds me of the words of Calvin who said that our hearts are idol factories. What do you think he meant by that?

Idolatry was the constant problem of Israel. They kept turning their backs on their God and turning towards false idols. They wanted to worship something they could see. Now God says that even the names of these idols will be banished from among them.

Idols had been given the people's devotion. But those who have been cleansed from their sin should now be in love with God. Anything which takes from us the affection which belongs to God alone should be banished from our lives.

Anyone whom the people of God love will be given their time. Anyone whom a believer loves will be given his affection. Anyone whom a church loves will be given its money. And anyone whom a Christian loves will occupy a large place in his or her thoughts. Today the Lord's people need to be asked, 'Is there anyone who claims more of your time, love, gifts and thoughts than the Lord Jesus Christ?' Anything which comes between God's people and the Lord is an idol and it needs to be torn down from its throne so that the Lord alone can be worshipped. — Michael Bentley, *Building for God's Glory: Haggai and Zechariah Simply Explained, Welwyn Commentary Series* (Darlington, England: Evangelical Press, 1989), 209.

11. Verse 7ff. What do we learn about Jesus from this section?

In contrast to the false prophets, the true Shepherd is presented in Zechariah 13:7. (Review Zech. 11 for the other "Shepherd" prophecies.) Jesus quoted part of this prophecy when He was on His way to Gethsemane with His disciples (Matt. 26:31), and He referred to it again when He was arrested in the garden (v. 56). Only Jesus the Messiah could the Father call "the man who is My fellow," that is, "the man who is My equal." (See John 10:30 and 14:9.) — Warren W. Wiersbe, *Be Heroic, "Be" Commentary Series* (Colorado Springs, CO: ChariotVictor Pub., 1997), 148.

12. Note the phrase, "strike the shepherd." What is this a reference to?

The most remarkable thing about verses 7 to 9 is that they describe God the Father as himself striking the Savior, just as Isaiah did in the well-known fifty-third chapter of his prophecy ("we considered him stricken by God, smitten by him, and afflicted," v. 4; "the Lord has laid on him the iniquity of us all," v. 6; "it was the Lord's will to crush him and cause him to suffer," v. 10). Zechariah says:

> "Awake, O sword, against my shepherd,
> against the man who is close to me!"
> declares the Lord Almighty.
> "Strike the shepherd,
> and the sheep will be scattered."
> Zechariah 13:7

This would not be so remarkable if it were spoken against the three false shepherds of Zechariah 11:8 or the foolish shepherd of 11:15-17. In fact, with no textual warrant whatever, some critical scholars have rearranged the text to place Zechariah 13:7-9 at the end of chapter 11—for just this reason. Judgment upon the wicked or derelict shepherds seems proper. But this is not a judgment against a false shepherd, but against one whom the verses themselves say is "close" to God and whom God himself identifies as "my shepherd."

Indeed, it is even stronger than this. For the words translated "close to me" are actually parallel to "my shepherd" and literally mean "my fellow" in the sense of "my close relation" or "blood associate." The great Bible commentator C. F. Keil writes of this word: "God would not apply this epithet to any godly or ungodly man whom he might have appointed shepherd over a nation. The idea of nearest one (or fellow) involves not only similarity in vocation, but community of physical or spiritual descent, according to which he whom God calls his neighbor cannot be a mere man, but can only be one who participates in the divine nature, or is essentially divine."

The solution to this problem is the incarnation, and the meaning of the verse is the atonement. It is God the Father striking his own Son, the Lord Jesus Christ, in our place as our sinbearer. It is Jesus suffering for us in order that we might be delivered from the wrath of God against sin and be released to serve the Lord effectively. — *Boice Expositional Commentary - An Expositional Commentary – The Minor Prophets, Volume 2: Micah-Malachi.*

13. Verse 7. What does it mean that the sheep will be scattered? When were the sheep scattered?

But there is also a wider meaning of this text as it relates to the scattering of the nation in A.D. 70 when Jerusalem was taken by the Romans. The Jews had smitten their Shepherd on the cross (Isa. 53:10), and this act of rejection led to the nation being scattered (Deut. 28:64; 29:24–25). Israel today is a dispersed people, but one day they shall be gathered; they are a defiled people, but one day they shall be cleansed. — Warren W. Wiersbe, *Be Heroic, "Be" Commentary Series* (Colorado Springs, CO: ChariotVictor Pub., 1997), 148.

14. Verse 8: "two thirds will be struck down and perish." What is that a reference to?

This scattering is to be intense and filled with suffering. In that day, "two-thirds will be struck down and perish" (v. 8). One can argue that this has already been fulfilled. Probably as many as two-thirds of the Jews living in Palestine perished at the time of the Roman victory in A.D. 70, when Jerusalem and Masada were overthrown, and at the time of the punishments associated with the Bar Cochba revolt a generation later. During the Middle Ages there were intense purges against the Jews, so much so that at the beginning of the sixteenth century, by reliable computation, there were only about one million Jews left in the entire world. Hitler exterminated six million Jews during World War II. — *Boice Expositional Commentary - An Expositional Commentary – The Minor Prophets, Volume 2: Micah-Malachi.*

15. Verse 9. Perhaps you have a study Bible with cross references in the center column. If so, what cross references do you find for verse 9?

I'd ask this question this way to teach people how they can use this tool to study the Bible for themselves.

Job 23:10 — But he knows the way that I take; when he has tested me, I will come forth as gold.

Pr 17:3 — The crucible for silver and the furnace for gold, but the LORD tests the heart.

Isa 48:10 — See, I have refined you, though not as silver; I have tested you in the furnace of affliction.

Mal 3:2 — But who can endure the day of his coming? Who can stand when he appears? For he will be like a refiner's fire or a launderer's soap.

Mal 3:3 — He will sit as a refiner and purifier of silver; he will purify the Levites and refine them like gold and silver. Then the LORD will have men who will bring offerings in righteousness,

Jas 1:12 — Blessed is the man who perseveres under trial, because when he has stood the test, he will receive the crown of life that God has promised to those who love him.

1Pe 1:6 — In this you greatly rejoice, though now for a little while you may have had to suffer grief in all kinds of trials.

1Pe 1:7 — These have come so that your faith--of greater worth than gold, which perishes even though refined by fire--may be proved genuine and may result in praise, glory and honor when Jesus Christ is revealed.

16. How does God refine us?

A happily married woman with two children lost both of them. They were buried in the same grave, and she went into a deep emotional collapse. For some years she became as weak and helpless as a little child. She had to be fed by members of her family who ministered to her. One day as her aunt, who was a joyful Christian, took her turn at feeding her, this woman who was unusually despondent that morning said, "Oh, Auntie, you say that God loves us. You say it, and you keep on saying it. I used to think that way, too, but if He loves us, why did He make me as I am?" The aunt, after kissing her gently, said with the wisdom of years, "He hasn't made you yet, child. He's making you now!"

> When through fiery trials thy pathway shall lie,
> My grace, all-sufficient, shall be thy supply;
> The flame shall not hurt thee; I only design
> Thy dross to consume and thy gold to refine.

— *Bible Illustrations – Illustrations of Bible Truths.*

17. How has God used the fire to refine you?

Pastors and their people must suffer. "Through many tribulations we must enter the kingdom of God" (Acts 14:22). "You yourselves know that we are destined for this" (1 Thess. 3:3). "The Lord disciplines the one he loves, and chastises every son he receives" (Heb. 12:6).

The afflictions suffered by the family of God are from the Heavenly Father for our good. Karolina Wilhelmina Sandell-Berg wrote the hymn, "Day by Day," in 1865, with the deeply Biblical words about God's sovereignty over our daily trials.

> He whose heart is kind beyond all measure
> Gives unto each day what He deems best—
> Lovingly, its part of pain and pleasure,
> Mingling toil with peace and rest.

This is a Biblical insight. Job and Paul have this in common: When struck by Satan, they felt the hand of God. Ultimately, their suffering was from the Lord, and they knew it.

The Lord said to Satan, "All that [Job] has is in your hand" (Job 1:12). But when the calamity struck, Job responded, "The Lord gave, and the Lord has taken away; blessed be the name of the Lord" (1:21). A second time the Lord said to

Satan, "Behold, [Job] is in your hand; only spare his life" (2:6). But when the horrid disease came and Job's wife urged him to curse God, Job replied, "Shall we receive good from God, and shall we not receive evil?" (2:10). And the inspired writer adds: "In all this Job did not sin with his lips."

Even if Satan is sometimes involved as the nearer cause of our calamities, it is not sin to see God as the more distant, primary, and ultimate cause. Satan's design is the destruction of faith (Job 2:5; 1 Thess. 3:5), but God's design is the deep cure of our soul, as the hymn, "How Firm a Foundation," says so powerfully:

> When through fiery trials thy pathways shall lie,
> My grace, all sufficient, shall be thy supply;
> The flame shall not hurt thee; I only design
> Thy dross to consume, and thy gold to refine.

Like Job, Paul recognized his thorn in the flesh as a "messenger of Satan" (2 Cor. 12:7) but designed by God for a gracious purpose: "to keep me from being too elated [conceited]."

Satan does not have free rein in the world and even less so in the family of God. Therefore, in our struggle with suffering, it will never be a sufficient comfort to say, "It is of Satan and not of God." The only genuine comfort will come from acknowledging that the all-powerful God has done it and that He is infinitely wise and infinitely loving to those who trust Him. William Cowper, who knew the darkness of depression, put it this way in his hymn, "God Moves in a Mysterious Way,"

> Judge not the Lord by feeble sense,
> But trust Him for His grace;
> Behind a frowning providence
> He hides a smiling face.
> His purposes will ripen fast,
> Unfolding every hour;
> The bud may have a bitter taste,
> But sweet will be the flower.

Brothers, We Are Not Professionals: A Plea to Pastors for Radical Ministry. Piper

18. What is it about fire that refines us?

What is accounted for is the quality of each man's work, "whether good or bad" (2 Cor. 5:10). The word here for "bad" is phaulos, which relates to the worth of something. Some works are worthless in terms of God's Kingdom and eternity. Others have great value. The fire of God's judgment will show which.

How will this take place? The key here is what fire does. It burns up anything flammable. Wood, hay, and straw go up in smoke. But gold and silver become finer.

When I visited Japan several years ago, I was astounded to see many "golden" idols in the Buddhist temples. But I was told that most were wood with a gilded paint veneer. On the other hand, I once viewed the treasures of King Tut's tomb. These were solid gold, beautiful, and valuable.

Imagine taking one of those Japanese idols and one of King Tut's treasures and subjecting both to fire. The idol would be reduced to char. But Tut's treasure, though melted down, would retain value as gold.

In the same way, I think that at the bema our works will go through a divine fire that determines their eternal value. Somehow this fire will consume anything not in line with the divine program, but it will refine anything that was right on target. Let me give an example.

Suppose a man, all full of smiles, gives a child a cup of water. From our perspective, that looks fine. But at the judgment seat of Christ, the fire heats up and we see what really happened. The man hadn't liked the child's begging, so he had given him the water to shut him up. He had put up a good front, but inside he had grumbled and cursed. The fire of truth reveals his heart. His worthless deed is consumed by the flames.

Another fellow gives a child a cup of water. He has no smile on his face. In fact, he's grimacing, as if he resents the effort. But at the judgment seat, we learn that he had suffered from back pain. That was why he had grimaced. Despite the pain, he had served selflessly. The fire of truth reveals his heart, and his worthy deed shines brilliantly.

In this sense, then, our whole lives will be subjected to Christ's fire. Whatever is selfish, mean, or petty will be consumed, but whatever is selfless, loving, and generous will grow purer and brighter.

At the bema our works will become evident to all. In 2 Cor. 5:10 Paul says we must all appear before the judgment seat of Christ. The word "appear" means to be made manifest, to become evident. Paul uses the same word in 1 Cor. 3:13, where he says each man's work "will be revealed with fire."

This judgment will take place in public, just like trials at the Roman bema. Our deeds will, in light of the accounting, examination, and testing, become plain to all. Everyone will see the justice of Christ's decision. No one will ever dispute it.

That's a scary idea, but I'm convinced that will be the nature of our appearance at the judgment seat of Christ. When everything is considered, all will conclude that Jesus' verdict is just. — *Discipleship Journal.*

19. Verse 9. It was true of Israel; it is true of us: we are His people. What are the implications? What is the application of this truth?

I love for my wedding ring to shine. About once a week I ask my friend who gets me up to use my toothpaste and toothbrush to scrub my ring. Real gold and diamonds can take a good scrubbing; they're not as delicate as we think. And when they're polished, my, they look lovely!

Malachi 3:16-17 talks about how the Lord has a book of remembrance in which the names of all those who meditate on him, who think about his name, are written down. He calls these people his jewels. How do we become jewels that gleam and shine in his sight? He says, "I will refine them like silver and test them like gold. They will call on my name and I will answer them; I will say, 'They are my people,' and they will say, The LORD is our God'" (Zech. 13:9).

Oh, that's what I want to be: a jewel that shines in his sight, a jewel that doesn't mind a good polishing now and then. I'm not as delicate as some people think, especially when God's grace sustains me.

Maybe you feel as if someone has taken a gigantic toothbrush and is scrubbing your soul raw. It hurts. And you wince at the pain, the disappointment. But take heart; there's a purpose.

Let me remind you: You're not as delicate as you think. You, as a believer, are a jewel, someone very precious to God. You're a diamond, you're silver, and you're gold. He promises that, as his jewel, he's going to shine you up. As silver is refined and as gold is tried, he will polish you bright so everyone will see you're a jewel.

Lord, help me to bring a willing spirit to you, one prepared to be polished even when it hurts. I want to be your jewel. — Joni Eareckson Tada, *More Precious than Silver: 366 Daily Devotional Readings* (Grand Rapids, MI: Zondervan, 2010).

20. What do you want to recall from today's conversation?

21. How can we support one another in prayer this week?

The closest that many believers come to group prayer is listening to a pastor pray from up front during the worship service. Prayer in the church today seems to be most often relegated to a few key leaders and perhaps a small set of people whose focus is to pray for the church.

Although we don't know for certain exactly how the New Testament church prayed together, it seems reasonable to believe that their experience of prayer was much more participatory than this. Phrases like "they all joined together constantly in prayer" (Acts 1:14), "they devoted themselves to the apostles' teaching . . . and to prayer" (Acts 2:42), "they raised their voices together in prayer" (Acts 4:24) and many others seem to portray prayer not as a spectator sport but as a participatory practice.

In many cases, the best way to move a church toward this participatory model of prayer is through the small group ministry. — Andrew Wheeler, *Together in Prayer: Coming to God in Community* (Westmont, IL: InterVarsity Press, 2010).

7 Minor Prophets, Lesson #7

Good Questions Have Small Groups Talking

www.joshhunt.com

Again, I'd email your group and ask them to do a little background reading. It is almost impossible to get fully up to speed on a passage like this with a little background reading. They don't need to do a lot of reading. Half an hour or so reading the notes in a study Bible will make the conversation a whole lot more interesting. Alternatively, you might email just a few of your readers and ask them to give a brief report on some of the background info.

Habakkuk 1, 2

OPEN

Let's each share your name and if you could ask God one question, what would it be?

DIG

1. **Look at your Bible's Table of Contents. What do you recall about any of the Minor Prophets?**

   The key to long term memory is review.

2. **Let's review . . . which of these came first?**

David or Daniel?

Abraham or Adam?

Joshua or Joseph?

Isaac or Isaiah?

Come up with your own pair, and the rest will put them in order.

3. **Introduction. Does your Bible have an introduction to Habakkuk? What is the big picture?**

Habakkuk addressed his book to God, not the people of Judah. In a frank dialogue with God, he discussed problems of suffering and justice. He could not understand how God could use Judah's enemies to judge his chosen people. But the book ends with Habakkuk's prayer of praise. — *The New International Version* (Grand Rapids, MI: Zondervan, 2011), Hab.

4. **What is Habakkuk feeling in verses 2 – 4?**

Have you been asking God questions about your life and the society in which you live? Why so much heartache, so much pain? Have you, like the prophet Habakkuk, become perplexed, distraught, saddened, grieved, and even angered at the injustices of today? What about the plight of the poor, the pain of the oppressed, the continual wickedness of humankind, and the hypocrisy and complacency of the Church? Have you cried in the midnight hour and asked God, "How long?" Have you thought, like Habakkuk, that maybe God just was not listening?

Are there problems in your life left unresolved, questions unanswered? Have you considered entering into the courtroom of the Kingdom of God to ask, "God, Your Honor, why? What's going on? What is the purpose? What's happening in my life?" — T. D. Jakes, *40 Days of Power* (Shippensburg, PA: Destiny Image, 2011).

5. How do you think God felt about Habakkuk questioning Him?

My best definition for prayer is simple: prayer is communicating with God. This straightforward concept can help put us at ease, especially when we realize that communication involves more than just talking. We communicate through music and body language and sculpting and painting and facial expressions and dancing and writing—even macramé! We each have our favorite modes of communication, and God is fluent in all of them. So if talking isn't your thing, you can still be good at praying.

Whether you pray by talking or by some other mode of communication, God most enjoys the prayer that is natural, direct, and simple. One of the most important qualities of effective communication is gut-level honesty. God hates it when we wear masks to the meeting, when our prayers become showy and inauthentic. Here are Jesus' instructions: "When you pray, do not be like the hypocrites, for they love to pray standing in the synagogues and on the street corners to be seen by men. I tell you the truth, they have received their reward in full...And when you pray, do not keep on babbling like pagans, for they think they will be heard because of their many words" (Matt. 6:5, 7).

The prayers of godly people recorded in Scripture are examples of straightforward honesty. When they were afraid, they told God about their fears. When they doubted, they doubted out loud in front of God. When they were angry, they let it rip. Under the reign of the evil King Jehoiakim, the nation of Judah was declining rapidly during a time of injustice, immorality, and violence. The prophet Habakkuk was convinced God wasn't doing what he should and cried out, "How long, O Lord, must I call for help, but you do not listen? Or cry out to you, 'Violence!' but you do not save? Why do you make me look at injustice? Why do you tolerate wrong?" (Hab. 1:2 – 3). You could call that a gut-level honest prayer, huh? Habakkuk wasn't the only one to talk honestly with God. Moses, Gideon, and Elijah all questioned God. Job even cursed the day God made him and said, "I loathe my very life; therefore I will give free rein to my complaint and speak out in the bitterness of my soul "(Job 10:1). Jesus never criticized prayers that were honest, only those that were long and showy.

As a parent, I'd much prefer my young children to climb up into my lap and speak honestly. "Daddy, I'm afraid of the dark. Would you help me?" Imagine the same child standing before me, addressing me thus: "Grand Omnipotent Father of the Household, I beseech your presence. Great provider of all I have, grant me thy presence through the long watches of the night, for lingering fears beset me—verily, until dawn's first rays at last light my heart with hope."

Odd picture. But that's exactly how many of us pray to our heavenly Father—or think we have to pray. — Craig Groeschel, *The Christian Atheist: When You Believe in God but Live as If He Doesn't Exist* (Grand Rapids, MI: Zondervan, 2010).

6. Is it appropriate for us to complain to God?

Did you know that such words were in the Bible? If so, do you wonder whether we are actually supposed to say them? Won't God get angry with us for daring to complain like this?

One year when my team and I were translating the Old Testament in West Africa, we happened to be working on Job and Jeremiah at the same time. The local translator on the project paused one day and floated a tense question: "It seems to me that these men and their constant complaining to God would eventually make him angry. Is it okay to complain to God?"

The answer came to me in a flash. "God can tolerate our complaints," I said. "Complaining to God is allowed with one major condition: we must continue to faithfully obey and follow him in spite of our suffering." That's why the complaining and grumbling of the Israelites in the wilderness aroused the cataclysmic anger of the Lord (for example, Numbers 11:1-3), but Jeremiah's and Job's complaints did not. In the face of agony, these two men never stopped loyally serving God. Their complaints demonstrated that they had faith —they offered faith-filled complaints. The Israelites' grumbling, on the other hand, was a demonstration of faithlessness.

The New Testament contains examples of this same principle. Paul implored God to remove his suffering: "There was given me a thorn in my flesh, a messenger of Satan, to torment me. Three times I pleaded with the Lord to take it away from me" (2 Corinthians 12:7-8). Yet Paul came to accept his pain as God's way "to keep [him] from becoming conceited" (verse 7) after he experienced indescribable supernatural visions and revelations.

Even Jesus experienced the pain of unanswered prayer. The night before he died, he prayed passionately, "Abba, Father, . . . everything is possible for you. Take this cup from me" (Mark 14:36). As he was dying on the cross, Jesus drew from one of the great prophetic complaints of the Old Testament (found in Psalm 22) as he cried out, "My God, my God, why have you forsaken me?" (Matthew 27:46).

Jesus had the faith to fulfill the prophecy, yet he would not deny the reality of the suffering involved. He showed his faith by reflecting on Scripture and having the courage to live out the fulfillment of that prophetic psalm. If relying on biblical, faith-filled words of complaint is okay for Jesus when he suffered, it's okay for us too.

Jesus and Paul didn't put a sunny, Christian facade on their suffering. There was no hollow, false perkiness at the Cross. They proved that complaints and faith are not mutually exclusive. — Greg Pruett and Max Lucado, *Extreme Prayer: The Impossible Prayers God Promises to Answer* (Carol Stream, IL: Tyndale, 2014).

7. Verse 5. How does God command Habakkuk to feel?

In the first two lines of verse 5, God responds to Habakkuk's complaint with great force: he employs four imperatives to make his point. And, interestingly, these imperative forms are all plural. The answer that God is giving to the prophet is not merely for him, but for all the covenant people. And the first thing he commands them to do is 'look'. The Lord is simply telling them to open their eyes and see what is really and truly happening in the world. God does not want his people to put their heads in the sand; rather, he desires that they should be aware of what is going on around them.

God then tells them to 'see'. This imperative is not a mere repetition of 'look' from the beginning of the verse. Rather, in this particular verbal stem (hiphil) in Hebrew, it means to give 'a careful, sustained, and favourable contemplation'. In other words, the Lord is telling his people not only to view the world rightly, but to think about it as well. Are you a thoughtful Christian? In this day of extreme busyness and activity, there appears to be little time for meditation and deliberation, for self-examination and world-examination, or for pondering the eternal questions. The old adage is correct that says, 'The probable reason some people get lost in thought is because it is unfamiliar territory to them'! Oswald Chambers encourages God's people when he says, 'To think is an effort; to think rightly is a great effort; and to think as a Christian ought to think is the greatest effort of a human soul.'2

Next, the Lord tells his people to 'wonder'. In Hebrew, this verb is reflexive and it bears the idea of a person being 'dumbfounded', or 'stunned'. It is used in Genesis 43:33 when Joseph's brothers sit before him and have a great feast in Egypt, and their response is one of 'amazement'. Have you ever been so awed and astonished by something that it made you silent? Wonders like the Grand Canyon, the Venus de Milo, a first view of the city of Jerusalem, or the birth of a child, can stun a person to silence.

And, finally, with the last imperative God calls on his people to 'be astounded'. This is the same verb just used at the beginning of the line; and, thus, the line literally reads: 'Astound yourselves and be astounded!' Repetition like this is emphatic. But why should the people of God be so dazzled and in wonder? — John D. Currid, *The Expectant Prophet: Habakkuk Simply Explained, Welwyn Commentary Series* (Darlington, England: EP Books, 2009), 41–43.

8. What do we learn about God from this?

I love the text from Habakkuk 1:5, which says, "Look among the nations and watch—be utterly astounded! For I will work a work in your days which you would not believe, though it were told you" (NKJV). God loves to do astounding things. And most of the time, He does those things in response to the prayers of His people. — David Jeremiah, *Prayer: The Great Adventure* (Sisters, OR: Multnomah Publishers, 1997), 133.

9. Verse 5ff. How did God reply to Habakkuk?

The answer that Habakkuk receives to his complaint (vv. 2–4) is here recorded in the form of a speech by God to the prophet. The Old Testament tells us that God does not hear every prayer (cf. Isa. 1:15) but he has heard faithful Habakkuk's persistent prayers (cf. Luke 18:1–8), and the answer God gives to those prayers is both comforting and confounding.

First, the Lord reassures the prophet that he is at work. In an age and a society where sinful human beings seem to rule the day and God seems totally absent from the field, God is nevertheless at work to realize his will for the world. The familiar hymn puts it very well:

> God is working his purpose out
> as year succeeds to year.
> God is working his purpose out,
> and the time is drawing near.
> Nearer and nearer draws the time,
> the time that shall surely be,
> When the earth shall be filled with the glory of God
> as the waters cover the sea (Arthur Campbell Ainger, 1894).

God is at work. God is the eternal worker. In a society where all the signs seem to read "Men Working," Habakkuk sees a vastly more impressive sign: "God Working" (Chappell, p. 77). God is not absent from the prophet's world. He has not written it off as a bad experiment. He is not ignorant of what is happening in Judah or throughout the Middle East. All is under his watchful eye, the subject of his concern, and he is at work in the midst of events to fulfill his good purpose. "My Father is working still, and I am working," Jesus told the Jews John 5:17). That is the ultimate word of comfort to anyone who despairs of society's evil, because God's working leads finally to good for all creation.

The nature of God's work that is told to Habakkuk seems to fly in the face of that assurance, however; for God tells the prophet that he is rousing the Babylonian Empire and its armies under Nebuchadnezzar (605/4–569. B.C.) to march through the Fertile Crescent, to capture nations (v. 6), to inflict violence on all in their path (v. 9), to overrun every fortified city (v. 10), and to take prisoners of war (v. 9). Their march will be swift (v. 6), dread and terrible (v. 7), sweeping through Palestine like the wind (v. 11), and none will be able to escape such force or to turn it aside. The scythe of Babylonia will cut down all in its path. And swinging the scythe—using it as an instrument of his purpose—will be God, the Lord over all nations and history. — Elizabeth Rice Achtemeier, *Nahum–Malachi, Interpretation, a Bible Commentary for Teaching and Preaching* (Atlanta, GA: John Knox Press, 1986), 37–38.

10. Verse 6. Who are the Chaldeans?

It starts out promising indeed. God tells Habakkuk to be patient, because God is about to do something incredible. "Be utterly astounded!" He says (Habakkuk 1:5). He also says, in a loose paraphrase, "If I tried to tell you, you wouldn't believe Me. But the wicked will get theirs."

So far, so good. But then comes the part that must have made Habakkuk choke. God drops this bomb: "I am raising up the Chaldeans" (Habakkuk 1:6).

The Chaldeans? Are You serious, Lord?

The Chaldeans, who came from the southern portion of Babylon, were the wickedest people on the map. God once sent Jonah to see them in Nineveh, and Jonah took off in the other direction. There was a reason any right-thinking prophet would want no part of that nation. As Jonah later said to God, it was unthinkable even to consider the Chaldeans escaping judgment. These were people who slew infants and offered them to idols. These were people who butchered their enemies in battle, far beyond the customs of warfare in that day. They seemed to have no conscience, no remorse, and no reluctance to overrun any nation in their sights. Indeed, the fear was that the Chaldeans would engulf the known world with their military power and their savagery.

But God hasn't forgotten any of this. As a matter of fact, He immediately catalogs all the atrocities and outrages of the Chaldeans. But He's going to be using them just the same.

Habakkuk is shaking his head, trying to take all this in. — David Jeremiah, *My Heart's Desire: Living Every Moment in the Wonder of Worship* (Nashville: Integrity Publishers, 2002), 152–153.

11. And how did Habakkuk reply to God?

God replied to Habakkuk that he was indeed going to take action. He was going to raise up the Babylonians, who would conquer and devastate Judah (1:5–11).

This provoked Habakkuk to raise a second question, which was in essence, "I admit that we are bad and deserve judgment, but the Babylonians are worse than we are. How can you, O God, allow the wicked to destroy those who are relatively more righteous?" (Hab. 1:12–17). — R.C. Sproul, *Before the Face of God: Book 3: A Daily Guide for Living from the Old Testament, electronic ed.* (Grand Rapids: Baker Book House; Ligonier Ministries, 1994).

12. How is Habakkuk feeling in this reply?

"Lord, this is not a good solution," Habakkuk insists. "I know we are wicked—but we are much more righteous than the Babylonians who will descend upon us like cruel fishermen, scoop us up like fish into their nets, and attribute the victory to their gods. You can't allow this, Lord!"

Now, Habakkuk is really struggling. Not only is God not doing what Habakkuk thinks He should be doing with the people of Judah, but He seems to be saying that the Babylonians are going to be victorious in their conquest. And that isn't fair at all, Habakkuk protests.

We all can relate to this. "How come they got a new house?" we ask. "Now, Lord, You know that I have devotions regularly and come to church faithfully. But I haven't seen them at church for weeks! Why are You blessing them—when you should be blessing me?"

Like us, Habakkuk was a questioner—but we are about to see him do something oh, so wise in chapter 2. — Jon Courson, *Jon Courson's Application Commentary: Volume Two: Psalms-Malachi* (Nashville, TN: Thomas Nelson, 2006), 858.

13. Habakkuk 2.1 What did Habakkuk do with his frustration? What is the lesson for us?

"I need an answer," said Habakkuk, "so I'm going to go up into my tower and seek My Father."

Please note three key components of this verse. The first is determination. When he needed an answer, Habakkuk said, "I will stand upon my watch." He didn't say, "Maybe I should spend some time with the Lord next week—or whenever it's convenient—or if I can break away from work—or if I can find some time." No, he said, "I need an answer and I'm determined to get one. I will seek the Lord."

The Lord promises that we shall find Him when we search for Him with all our heart (Jeremiah 29:13). But so often we lack determination. Oh, there's an acknowledgement in our minds that we should seek the Lord. There's an intention that we probably will seek the Lord sometime. But we don't get answers to the questions with which we wrestle because we lack this key component of determination.

Second, notice Habakkuk's isolation. He got away from his telephone, radio, and television and went up into a tower. He got away from all the distractions that would otherwise bombard him. I believe we don't hear the voice of God because there are so many other voices constantly ringing in our ears. If you really want to hear from the Lord, there is no alternative to a quiet time, a quiet place, and a quiet heart.

Finally, notice Habakkuk's expectation. He said, "I will see what the Lord will say to me," not, "what He might say to me," not, "what I hope He will say to me," not, "what I wish He would say to me," but "what He will say to me."

Hebrews 11:6 declares that without faith, it is impossible to please God for he that comes to God must believe that He is and that He is a rewarder of them that diligently seek Him. There are many ways to please God—but none apart from faith. If you don't believe God is going to speak to you and deal with you, you're not going to hear anything from Him.

How do you know if God will speak to you or not? Here is a very simple test: when you seek the Lord, do you have a journal with you—a pencil and paper before you? You see, if I don't really expect God to speak, I'll just kind of show up, casually slumped in my chair, saying, "Wonder if there's anything in the Word for me today... Probably not..."

We adopt a laid-back mentality in seeking God and then wonder why we never hear from Him. But those who expect to hear from God have pencil and paper in hand. They are on the edge of their chair or on their knees in a posture of expectancy rather than in a spirit of complacency and lethargy.

Habakkuk said, "I am going to seek God. I will get away and I will hear what He has to say to me." That's the kind of faith that honors God. That's the kind of faith that clears the wax of the world out of the ears of the inner man. — Jon Courson, *Jon Courson's Application Commentary: Volume Two: Psalms-Malachi* (Nashville, TN: Thomas Nelson, 2006), 858–859.

14. Habakkuk 2.2. What did God tell Habakkuk to write down the revelation? What is the application for us?

A tangible testament of God's commandments was so important to him that he entrusted Moses to be keeper of it and to deliver the message on the tablets to the people of Israel. God could have easily told Moses to commit the Ten Commandments to memory, but he knew a written record would last longer and be an everlasting reminder of his faithfulness to future generations. So he inscribed those blocks of stone with the words the Israelites were to live by. And the same holds true today. Just as our words have power when spoken, they have power when written down as well. In order to obtain success, we must write our goals down.

What do you want? A promotion? A new house? A better marriage? Then write it down. It's been said that people who write down their goals achieve them faster than those who don't. Apparently, there is a connection between putting ideas, thoughts, goals, and dreams in writing and having them come to fruition. In some professions, written goal setting is mandatory, because companies know it works.

When I joined Weight Watchers, I was asked to set—and attain—5 and 10 percent weight-loss goals during my weight-loss journey. I was openly applauded and rewarded when I reached them—and that felt great! And no wonder: the written word has biblical roots, as evidenced in Habakkuk 2:2.

I believe that when you write down your goals, dreams, and visions, something is released in the spiritual realm. God wants to bless you abundantly as you seek his will for your life. "Delight yourself in the Lord and he will give you the desires of your heart. Commit your way to the Lord; trust in him and he will do this" (Ps. 37:4–5). — Carol M. Mackey, *Sistergirl Devotions: Keeping Jesus in the Mix on the Job* (Grand Rapids, MI: Baker, 2010).

15. What good came from Habakkuk writing things down?

We wouldn't be studying this book today had Habakkuk not obeyed God's orders and written down what God had told him and shown him. This writing was to be permanent so that generation after generation could read it. It was also to be plain, written so that anybody could read it, and it was to be public so that even somebody running past the tablets on display could get the message immediately. Habakkuk wasn't the only person in Judah who needed this message, and it was his obligation to share it. — Warren W. Wiersbe, *Be Amazed, "Be" Commentary Series* (Wheaton, IL: Victor Books, 1996), 117.

16. What are some things we would do well to write down?

Habakkuk 2:2 tells us to "Write the vision and make it plain on tablets, that he may run who reads it" (NKJV). There is power in writing things down. When you preach on evangelism and then take the time to have people write down the names of friends who are on their hearts, they will be significantly more likely to see and seize opportunities to invite those people to church.

As we approach our Easter big day, I always use Palm Sunday to challenge our people to write down the names of ten unchurched friends they would like to invite to the Easter services. For most other big days, I challenge everyone a week or two in advance to write down the names of three unbelieving friends they will invite. This is also a great time to encourage members and regular attenders to continue making unchurched friends. — Nelson Searcy and Jennifer Dykes Henson, *Ignite: How to Spark Immediate Growth in Your Church* (Grand Rapids, MI: Baker Books, 2009), 97–98.

17. How does Habakkuk seem to see himself in Habakkuk 2.1? What is the lesson for us?

The prophet saw himself as a watchman on the walls of Jerusalem, waiting for a message from God that he could share with the people. In ancient days, the watchmen were responsible to warn the city of approaching danger, and if they weren't faithful, their hands would be stained with the blood of the people who died (Ezek. 3:17–21; 33:1–3). It was a serious responsibility.

The image of the watchman carries a spiritual lesson for us today. As God's people, we know that danger is approaching, and it's our responsibility to warn people to "flee from the wrath to come" (Matt. 3:7). If we don't share the Gospel with lost sinners, then their blood may be on our hands. We want to be able to say with Paul, "Therefore I testify to you this day that I am innocent of the blood of all men" (Acts 20:26, NKJV). — Warren W. Wiersbe, *Be Amazed, "Be" Commentary Series* (Wheaton, IL: Victor Books, 1996), 116–117.

18. Verse 4. What does it mean to be puffed up?

The Babylonians were "puffed up" with pride over their military might and their great achievements. They had built an impressive empire which they were sure was invincible. The words of Nebuchadnezzar express it perfectly: "Is not this great Babylon, that I have built for a royal dwelling by my mighty power for the honor of my majesty?" (Dan. 4:30, NKJV)

But Nebuchadnezzar and the Babylonians aren't the only ones puffed up with pride and self-sufficiency. This is the condition of most of the people in today's society who belong to the world and live for the world. The Apostle John warns us against "the pride [vain glory] of life" that belongs to this present evil world system which is against God and without God (1 John 2:15–17). — Warren W. Wiersbe, *Be Amazed, "Be" Commentary Series* (Wheaton, IL: Victor Books, 1996), 118.

19. What bad things come to the puffed up?

Besides puffing them up, what else does pride do to people? It twists them inwardly, for the soul of the unbeliever is "not upright," which means his inner appetites are crooked and sinful. He delights in the things that God abhors, the things

God condemns in the five "woes" in this chapter. One of the chief causes of the corruption in this world is what Peter calls "lust" (2 Peter 1:4), which simply means "evil desires, passionate longing." Were it not for the base appetites of people, longing to be satisfied but never satisfied, the "sin industries" would never prosper.

Pride also makes people restless: they're never satisfied (Hab. 2:5). That's why they're given over to wine, never at rest, never satisfied. They're constantly seeking for some new experience to thrill them or some new achievement to make them important. Pride makes us greedy. The Babylonians weren't satisfied with what they had; they coveted even more land and wealth, and therefore set their course to conquer every nation that stood in their way. More than one king or dictator in history has followed this resolve, only to discover that it leads to disappointment, ruin, and death. — Warren W. Wiersbe, *Be Amazed, "Be" Commentary Series* (Wheaton, IL: Victor Books, 1996), 118–119.

20. Verse 4 speaks of the just (NKJV). What does it mean to be just? What do we learn about being just from this passage?

The just. Now for the contrast: "The just shall live by his faith" (v. 4b; see Rom. 1:17; Gal. 3:11; Heb. 10:38). This is the first of three wonderful assurances that God gives in this chapter to encourage His people. This one emphasizes God's grace, because grace and faith always go together. Habakkuk 2:14 emphasizes God's glory and assures us that, though this world is now filled with violence and corruption (Gen. 6:5, 11–13), it shall one day be filled with God's glory. The third assurance is in Habakkuk 2:20 and emphasizes God's government. Empires may rise and fall, but God is on His holy throne, and He is King of Kings and Lord of Lords.

"The just shall live by his faith" was the watchword of the Reformation, and they may well be the seven most important monosyllables in all of church history. It was verse 4, quoted in Romans 1:17, that helped to lead Martin Luther into the truth of justification by faith. "This text," said Luther, "was to me the true gate of Paradise."

Justification is the gracious act of God whereby He declares the believing sinner righteous and gives that believing sinner a perfect standing in Jesus Christ. The "just" person isn't someone who has met all of God's requirements by means of good works, "For by the works of the law shall no flesh be justified" (Gal. 2:19; see Rom. 4:5). "For if righteousness comes through the law, then Christ died in vain" (Gal. 2:21, NKJV).

Our Lord's Parable of the Pharisee and the Publican makes it clear that no amount of religious effort can save a lost sinner (Luke 18:9–14). We can't justify ourselves before God because we stand with the whole world, guilty and condemned before His throne (Rom. 3:19). All we can do is put saving faith in Jesus Christ and His work on the cross, because that is the only way to be saved. "Therefore, being justified by faith, we have peace with God through our Lord Jesus Christ" (Rom. 5:1). — Warren W. Wiersbe, *Be Amazed, "Be" Commentary Series* (Wheaton, IL: Victor Books, 1996), 119–120.

21. Summary. What did you learn today? What do you want to recall from today's conversation?

22. How can we support one another in prayer this week?

7 Minor Prophets, Lesson #8

Good Questions Have Small Groups Talking

www.joshhunt.com

Again, I'd email your group and ask them to do a little background reading. It is almost impossible to get fully up to speed on a passage like this with a little background reading. They don't need to do a lot of reading. Half an hour or so reading the notes in a study Bible will make the conversation a whole lot more interesting. Alternatively, you might email just a few of your readers and ask them to give a brief report on some of the background info.

Habakkuk 3

OPEN

Let's each share your name and one thing that seems to be on your mind these days.

DIG

1. **Refresh our memories. What is the book of Habakkuk about?**

Habakkuk ministered during the final "death throes" of the nation of Judah. Although God had repeatedly called the nation to repentance, Judah stubbornly refused to change her sinful ways.

The prophet, knowing the hardheartedness of his countrymen, asked God how long such an intolerable condition could continue. God replied that He would use the brutal Babylonians as His chastening rod upon the wayward nation—an announcement that sent the prophet to his knees. How could God use a nation more wicked than Judah to punish Judah? God answered that, in His time, He would also punish the Babylonians.

Habakkuk did not entirely understand or celebrate God's plan, but He acknowledged that the just in any generation live by faith (Hab. 2:4). So he would leave the situation in God's holy hands. Habakkuk concluded his little book by praising God's wisdom, even though he did not fully grasp God's mysterious ways. — Charles F. Stanley, *The Charles F. Stanley Life Principles Bible: New King James Version* (Nashville, TN: Nelson Bibles, 2005), Hab.

2. **What was the mood in chapter one?**

The prophet Habakkuk, of course, was a fist shaker. He was one of those who dared to question God, a minor prophet with major questions. He carried on a dialogue with the Creator that constitutes his entire book in the Old Testament. It's a great pity that his conversation with God lies in one of those neglected neighborhoods of the Scriptures. We should travel there more often. — David Jeremiah, *My Heart's Desire: Living Every Moment in the Wonder of Worship* (Nashville: Integrity Publishers, 2002), 150–151.

3. Habakkuk 3.2. What is Habakkuk feeling in this verse?

No verse reveals more clearly than this one that Habakkuk's concern is not with his own ineffectiveness as a prophet. Habakkuk does not pray here, "Lord, prosper my work." He prays, "Lord, renew thy work." He wants God's purpose to be fulfilled, God's work on earth to be done, God's actions to be seen clearly by faith in the passages of history. This prophet concentrates on God and not on human beings. And so should the church when it uses this text. — Elizabeth Rice Achtemeier, *Nahum–Malachi, Interpretation, a Bible Commentary for Teaching and Preaching* (Atlanta, GA: John Knox Press, 1986), 54–55.

4. What is the application of this verse for our lives?

The Kingdom of God—that is the church's proper concern, is it not?

> Let goods and kindred go,
> This mortal life also;
> The body they may kill:
> God's truth abideth still;
> His Kingdom is forever ("A Mighty Fortress Is Our God").

There is our focus—the kingship of God. What does it matter if some cause is defeated, if some nation totters, if some suffering is borne? The question in the midst of it all is, Has the time of the Kingdom drawn nearer? Has God's purpose been advanced? Is his banner still on high? The church's goal is every knee bent and every tongue confessing Christ's lordship. The church's concern is the glory of the Lord known over all the earth. The church's cause is one Lord, one faith, one baptism, one God and Father of us all, in all and through all. And so the church's prayer is and must ever be, "O Lord, in the midst of the years, renew thy work. Bring in thy Kingdom on this earth, even as it is in heaven."

It is quite certain that we ourselves cannot achieve that goal. There is the delusion abroad in our time that the achievement of liberation for the oppressed in society, or the sharing of wealth with the poor, or the achievement of nuclear disarmament will usher in the Kingdom of God. But noble and necessary as they may be, human causes, in whatever age, are always marred by that creaturely pride and selfishness that war against the Creator. And finally God himself will have to establish his reign in the hearts and societies of sinful human beings, transformed to accord with his lordship. In the power of the Spirit, we can work in accord with God's purpose, to be sure. We can choose to promote it, and not oppose it. But we cannot finally achieve that salvation that only God can give.

The coming of the Kingdom will mean salvation (cf. 3:13), that is, God's abundant life. On the way to the achievement of his goal, God puts down the wicked and rids the earth of the proud evil that opposes his rule. But when the Kingdom comes, evil is gone and good alone remains. — Elizabeth Rice Achtemeier, *Nahum–Malachi, Interpretation, a Bible Commentary for Teaching and Preaching* (Atlanta, GA: John Knox Press, 1986), 55–56.

5. **Verse 2. Note the word "awe." Can you think of other verses that speak of the awe of God? If you have smart phone, do a search.**

NEHEMIAH 9:6 You alone are the LORD. You made the heavens, even the highest heavens, and all their starry host, the earth and all that is on it, the seas and all that is in them. You give life to everything, and the multitudes of heaven worship you.

PSALM 27:4 One thing I ask from the LORD, this only do I seek: that I may dwell in the house of the LORD all the days of my life, to gaze on the beauty of the LORD and to seek him in his temple.

PSALM 71:5-6 You have been my hope, Sovereign LORD, my confidence since my youth. From birth I have relied on you; you brought me forth from my mother's womb. I will ever praise you.

PSALM 116:1-2 I love the LORD, for he heard my voice; he heard my cry for mercy. Because he turned his ear to me, I will call on him as long as I live.

HABAKKUK 3:2 LORD, I have heard of your fame; I stand in awe of your deeds, LORD. Repeat them in our day, in our time make them known; in wrath remember mercy. — Bill Hybels, *Simplify: Ten Practices to Unclutter Your Soul* (Carol Stream, IL: Tyndale, 2014).

6. **R.C. Sproul has written that our soul craves to feel awe. What do you think he means by that?**

In his famous Republic, Plato spoke of prisoners in a cave, shut off from the outside world, limited in their vision to gazing at shadows on the wall. For these men the shadows were their window on reality. In time they began to mistake the shadows for the reality. The cave served as a parable for Plato to describe the difference between opinion and knowledge, between transcendent truth and its imperfect earthly copy.

Modern man has returned to the cave. We have locked ourselves in a dark place where the windows are blackened and the door is barred. We seal the cracks lest light might seep through from above and reveal the ephemeral quality of our eyes. We dance with the shadows as we stumble in the dark.

When people shut themselves off from the transcendent they become blind to ultimate truth. We lose sight of the sublime, we become indifferent to wonder. The sense of awe is extinguished and we are reduced to the contempt of the familiar. We are surface-bound creatures, content to live by the creed "What you see is what you get." The depth-dimension of reality eludes us not so much because it is inaccessible but because we are not interested in it, or even more seriously, hostile to it. It is what Calvin meant when he said that we are like people walking blindfolded through a glorioustheater.

When Rudolf Otto published his work on the holiness of God, the original German title of the book was Das Heilige. A direct translation of this title into English would read simply, The Holy. However, when the book was rendered into English the title that appeared was, The Idea of the Holy. I wonder if Otto, himself, knew of this title. I can't imagine that he would have approved of it. Otto wasn't concerned about the idea of the Holy; he was consumed by the reality of the Holy.

For Plato there was no essential difference between idea and reality. Formodern man there is a profound difference. For us, concepts follow an awareness of something. An infant does not think with words. The infant knows no words. He must acquire verbal skills. He learns a language, which is a system of sounds related to concepts or ideas that are associated with perceived reality. He begins not with words or concepts; he begins with awareness.

We don't speak much about transcendence. Indeed, the word itself is not active in many people's vocabulary. The concept tends to be ignored. That is because we repress our awareness of the transcendent.

Rabbi Abraham Heschel, in his God in Search of Man: A Philosophy of Judaism, decries the loss of wonder and awe in modern man. He writes: "The surest way to suppress our ability to understand the meaning of God and the importance of worship is to take things for granted. Indifference to the sublime wonder of living is the root of sin." — R.C. Sproul, Tabletalk: Selected Articles from Tabletalk Magazine, electronic ed. (Ligonier, PA: Ligonier Ministries, 2000).

7. What does it feel like to experience awe?

Otto analyzes the notion of tremendum by isolating its constituent elements. First is the element of awfulness—not awful in the sense of being bad but in the literal sense of being "full of awe." This awfulness is of a peculiar nature. The emotion of fear is closely connected with it, but it is not quite the same. We derive words like tremor and tremble from the concept of tremendum. The fear associated with the element of awfulness is one that produces tremors or trembling. We think of Søren Kierkegaard's words about Abraham in his Fear and Trembling, in which he scrutinized the peculiar kind of "awful dread that is experienced in the presence of God." Or we think of the black spiritual "Were You There When They Crucified My Lord?" with its ominous refrain, "Sometimes it causes me to tremble, tremble, tremble."

Otto notes the close relationship between the awfulness element and the Greek term sebastos. This title in its Latin form is augustus. He notes the early Christian antipathy to the use of the title augustus with reference to any man, even the emperor. "They felt that to call a man sebastos was to give a human being a name proper only to the numen, to rank him by the category proper only to the numen, and that it therefore amounted to a kind of idolatry."

This awe is a sort of reverent fear that produces a shuddering kind of dread. The development of the usage of the term awful suggests that there is a strong negative feeling associated with the experience of religious awe. The term awful is now used almost exclusively as a synonym for bad or very bad.

The second element of the tremendum is the element of "overpoweringness." Otto links this awareness of might and power with the Latin majestas. Confrontation with this majestic power evokes a sense of impotence, inadequacy, and general nothingness. — R.C. (Robert Charles) Sproul, *If There's a God, Why Are There Atheists?: Why Atheists Believe in Unbelief, Revised edition of the book The psychology of Atheism.* (Wheaton, IL: Tyndale House Publishers, 1978).

8. Can you describe a time when you felt in awe of God?

Otto coined a special term for the holy. He called it the mysterium tremendum. A simple translation of this concept is the "awful mystery." Otto described it like this:

The feeling of it may at times come sweeping like a gentle tide, pervading the mind with a tranquil mood of deepest worship. It may pass over into a more set and lasting attitude of the soul, continuing, as it were, thrillingly vibrant and resonant, until at last it dies away and the soul resumes its "profane," non-religious mood of everyday experience. It may burst in sudden eruption up from the depths of the soul with spasms and convulsions, or lead to the strangest excitements, to intoxicated frenzy, to transport, and to ecstasy. It has its wild and demonic forms and can sink to an almost grisly horror and shuddering. It has its crude barbaric antecedents and early manifestations, and again it may be developed into something beautiful and pure and glorious. It may become the hushed, trembling, and speechless humility of the creature in the presence of—whom or what? In the presence of that which is a mystery inexpressible and above all creatures. [Rudolph Otto, The Idea of the Holy (Oxford University Press, 1950), pp. 12-13.]

Otto spoke of the tremendum (awe-fulness) because of the fear the holy provokes in us. The holy fills us with a kind of dread. We use expressions like "My blood ran icy cold" or "My flesh crept."

We think of the Negro spiritual: "Were you there when they crucified my Lord?" The refrain of the song says: "Sometimes it causes me to tremble . . . tremble . . . tremble."

We tend to have mixed feelings about the holy. There is a sense in which we are at the same time attracted to it and repulsed by it. Something draws us toward it while at the same time we want to run away from it. We can't seem to decide which way we want it. Part of us yearns for the holy while part of us despises it. We can't live with it and we can't live without it.

Our attitude toward the holy is close to our attitude toward ghost stories and horror movies. Children beg their parents to tell them ghost stories until they get so frightened they beg them to stop. I hate to take my wife to scary movies. She loves to see them until she sees them—or, I should say, doesn't see them. We go through the same pattern each time. First she clutches my arm and digs her fingernails into my flesh. The only relief I get is when she removes her hands from my arm so she can use both hands to cover her eyes.

The next step is when she leaves her seat and goes to the rear of the theater where she can stand with her back against a solid wall. There she can be sure nothing is going to jump out from behind her and grab her. The final step is when she leaves the theater altogether and seeks refuge in the lobby. Yet she tells me that she loves to go to such movies. (There must be a theological illustration in there somewhere.) — R. C. Sproul, *The Holiness of God* (Wheaton, IL: Tyndale House Publishers, 1993).

9. Verse 16. How is Habakkuk feeling now?

Habakkuk is sobered. Earlier, he said, "Lord, do something." Now, he says, "Lord, I tremble when I see what You will do. I asked for judgment in chapter 1, but I spoke quickly. Now I see that when You step, mountains melt; when You walk, the earth quakes." — Jon Courson, *Jon Courson's Application Commentary: Volume Two: Psalms-Malachi* (Nashville, TN: Thomas Nelson, 2006), 868–869.

10. Has your heart ever pounded as you heard from God? Who has a story?

His 'heart pounded'. The Hebrews regard the 'heart' or belly (lower abdomen) as the seat of the emotions, the innermost part of an individual (cf. Proverbs 20:27; Isaiah 16:11). Habakkuk's heart 'pounded' or trembled with fear and astonishment. His whole inward self vibrated at the thought of God's wrath. He was torn by spasms, overpowered by feelings of dismay, terrified with forebodings. His 'lips' palpitated or chattered like teeth to such an extent that he could hardly fulfil the prophetic office and utter the terrors he heard.

The strongest part of his body ('my bones') was smitten with a rottenness that consumed his strength and languished his spirits (cf. Proverbs 12:4; 14:30). An uncontrollable weakness seemed to sap his vigour. His 'legs [lower limbs] trembled' as if shaken by an earthquake. He could only totter and not properly support himself. He was ready to collapse. From top to bottom he was convulsed by terror. — Tim Shenton, *Habakkuk: An Expositional Commentary, Exploring the Bible*

Commentary (Leominster, UK: Day One Publications, 2007), 85–86.

11. Verses 17 – 19. This is one of the most beautiful—and significant—passages in the Bible. The language is a little archaic. Paraphrase it in your own words.

Aren't those words magnificent? This is absolutely one of my favorite passages in all the Word of God. The prophet is saying, "Our crops may fail. Our flocks may wander. No matter what happens, I will praise God. And the day will come when He will take me to the highest peaks of joy."

This is the ultimate expression of faith and worship. Habakkuk recognizes that times may be good, times may be bad, and circumstances may waver—but none of it has anything to do with our praise and worship. Our adoration remains constant because He remains constant. This is how Job can lose his family, his friends, his home, and his every possession, yet love God all the more deeply. This is how a man can see his wife violently taken from him, body broken in a ditch with their unborn child, and rise to proclaim that God is no less faithful, no less loving.

This is why those who don't know God are consumed by the fires of life, yet those who trust God are refined by those same fires. It's the power of knowledge and trust. —David Jeremiah, *My Heart's Desire: Living Every Moment in the Wonder of Worship* (Nashville: Integrity Publishers, 2002), 164.

12. Look at the very last line of Habakkuk. What is that telling us?

One of the most intriguing elements of this book is that it seems to have musical origins. Habakkuk 3:19 tells us it was written for the "chief musician," and the only other place where we find the musical annotation "selah" is the Psalms. So what we have here seems to be a kind of duet between God and His questioning child, as recorded for the people's use. In its opening overture, at least, it is the music of misery.

Yet it is also the source of a certain joy, for this book is the ultimate source text of the Protestant Reformation. It is in Habakkuk 2:4b where we read, "The just shall live by his faith," the battle cry of the movement started by Martin Luther and John Calvin that rediscovered the priesthood of every believer. — David Jeremiah, *My Heart's Desire: Living Every Moment in the Wonder of Worship* (Nashville: Integrity Publishers, 2002), 151.

13. Verse 18. How is Habakkuk feeling now?

G. Campbell Morgan, a conservative expositor of the Word from the last generation, surprised me when he wrote about Habakkuk's song:

> I hope I shall produce no shock when I translate verse 18 literally. Take the first Hebrew word [of verse 18] and express it quite literally, and this is it: "I will jump for joy in the Lord." Take the second of the words and translate it with equal literalness and this is it: "I will spin around in the God of my salvation."

In a moment of deep discouragement, Habakkuk used music to lift himself up, even to the point where he said, "I am ready to jump for joy to the God of my salvation, and spin around because of who God is." — David Jeremiah, *The Power of Encouragement* (Sisters, OR: Multnomah Books, 1997), 62–63.

14. Describe a time when you have felt as Habakkuk is feeling.

Over the years, God has used music again and again to minister to my heart, to encourage me. Once when my wife was seriously ill and the doctors could not find the cause of her illness, someone gave me a tape of Andre Crouch's great chorus, "Through it all, I've learned to trust in Jesus, I've learned to trust in God." I played that song over and over until I wore out the tape.

Music is one of God's most blessed gifts and you can encourage yourself through song. — David Jeremiah, *The*

Power of Encouragement (Sisters, OR: Multnomah Books, 1997), 63.

15. We always want to read the Bible for application. What is the application of Habakkuk 3.17 – 19?

Habakkuk, you see, made a choice. His country was in turmoil; his God had no answers that made sense. When there was no explanation for things that he could wrap his mind around, the prophet said, "I do have one option: I can praise God. The world around me may be in turmoil, yet though all of it falls apart, I will rejoice in the God of my salvation."

That same choice faces you. You can demand all the answers, neatly gift-wrapped. You can insist that God quickly resolve every trial and injustice in your life. You can hold out for the world, and your life within it, to become suddenly fair and rational, though they've never been so in the first place.

Or you can choose to lift up your eyes to the heavens, pour out your tears and grief and anger, and say in the very midst of them, "God, I have no clue what this turmoil is all about or where it is leading, but this is my resolution: I will put my trust in You, and I will praise You with all of my heart, unconditionally!"

The same God who has been there for you in the past is the God who is going to be there for you in the future. He will bring resolution in His own time, according to His own purposes. We become preoccupied with our circumstances; God is preoccupied with our character. He will allow the tough times for the higher good of our character until He is finished with the great work that is invisible to our earthly eyes.

And yet, you can be encouraged. God never waits too long. He is never late, nor does He lose control. He makes no misjudgments or mistakes. Next time you're in that ceaseless tunnel, and there seems to be no light to lead you on, think of Sharon Paul's words: "Even on my darkest days, I can still say I've seen Jesus. I've seen Him with the eyes of my spirit, even if the eyes of my mind and heart are blinded. I'm so grateful that He is my Savior."

The writer of Psalm 13 concluded, "I will sing to the LORD, for he has been good to me" (NIV). I hope you've learned the joy of singing when God delays. — David Jeremiah, *When Your World Falls Apart: See Past the Pain of the Present* (Nashville, TN: Thomas Nelson Publishers, 2007), 101–102.

16. How. How do we rejoice in the Lord when "the fig tree does not bud"?

Today's Scripture from the book of Habakkuk is a magnificent description of a heart that holds on to joy by faith. The prophet looked around him, and knew he was in a season of deep trouble and need. But in spite of all the negative circumstances, he said, "I will rejoice in the Lord. I will be joyful in my God."

Solomon said, "For the happy heart, life is a continual feast" (Proverbs 15:15, NLT). The psalmist wrote that in the presence of God there is fullness of joy, and at His right hand pleasures forevermore (see Psalm 16:11). Jesus said, "My purpose is to give them a rich and satisfying life" (John 10:10, NLT). God wants us to experience joy as believers—not a fickle happiness that depends on circumstances or changes with the wind direction, but a joy that remains in spite of what may be taking place around us.

Anyone can be relatively happy when things are going well. But when you face adversity or sickness or hardship and then rejoice, you show that something supernatural has occurred in your life. In fact, you show yourself to be a real Christian. This is a unique trait of believers—that we can rejoice when things go wrong.

How do we do it? We find the key in Philippians 4:4: "Rejoice in the Lord always. Again I will say, rejoice!" Paul didn't say to rejoice in circumstances. Rather, he said to rejoice in the Lord. In other words, God is still on the throne. You're still going to heaven. You're still forgiven. God still has a plan for your life; He has not abandoned you. We need to take joy in the Lord always. That is the key. I recognize that in spite of what I may be going through right now, His plans for me are still good. And He will never leave or forsake me. — Greg Laurie, *Daily Hope for Hurting Hearts: A Devotional* (Dana Point, CA: Kerygma Publishing—Allen David Books, 2011).

17. Verse 19 is the basis of a famous devotional book—Hinds Feet in High Places. What does that mean, hinds feet in high places. (See KJV.)

Habakkuk's journey as a prophet had grown treacherous. Around him, all other ground was sinking sand. But these five places, he knew, were secure. We can take our stand on these firm foundations. We can keep moving when nothing around us seems to be dependable. How many times have I done the same? Too many to count, and I hope you've done likewise.

As we are faced with some terrible crisis, some awful calamity, we stop to review the lowest common denominators of faith. Death is staring us in the face—but He is eternal. We're surrounded by so much that is wicked—but He is holy. The rats keep winning the rat race—but He appoints them for judgment. When it seems as if the whole world is sinking into the muck, we need not remain in the valley. **We can set hind's feet on high places, like the deer**. We can lift up our eyes, and our spirits and confidence will follow. Habakkuk's name means "the one who embraces," but it also means "the one who clings." We can cling to God for dear life, and we can do it by setting foot on each of these principles. — David Jeremiah, *My Heart's Desire: Living Every Moment in the Wonder of Worship* (Nashville: Integrity Publishers, 2002), 154–155.

18. What do we learn about following God from this verse?

Violence and destruction surrounded the prophet Habakkuk as his disobedient nation, Judah, fell under the heel of the warlike Chaldeans. Though he called out to God, the faithful prophet seemed to get no answer.

Habakkuk recognized God's judgment in this attack by a pagan people, yet he still looked to his Lord for mercy. This verse of hopeful words declares that Habakkuk's strength still came from the same Lord who used His power to humble His people.

Are we feeling tired today? Drained spiritually and financially? Do the warriors of disease, depression, or despair attack us? Let's follow in Habakkuk's footsteps: When destruction stares us in the face, let's make God our strength.

Our Lord's power offers us a firm footing, no matter what dangerous places we travel through. He will carry us safely over high mountain trails or through deep swamps.

Though He sometimes sets a difficult path before us, God does not leave us to walk alone. In His strength, wherever we go, we cannot fall. — Barbour Publishing Inc and Brigitta Nortker, *3-Minute Devotions for Women: Daily Devotional* (purple) (Uhrichsville, OH: Barbour, 2013).

19. What do you want to recall from today's conversation?

20. How can we support one another in prayer this week?

7 Minor Prophets, Lesson #9

Good Questions Have Small Groups Talking

www.joshhunt.com

Again, I'd email your group and ask them to do a little background reading. It is almost impossible to get fully up to speed on a passage like this with a little background reading. They don't need to do a lot of reading. Half an hour or so reading the notes in a study Bible will make the conversation a whole lot more interesting. Alternatively, you might email just a few of your readers and ask them to give a brief report on some of the background info.

Haggai

OPEN

Let's each share your name and one thing that seems to be on your mind these days.

DIG

1. **Overview. Did you get a chance to look at Haggai this week? What is the big picture? What is Haggai about?**

   Israelite excitement over returning to the land was short-lived. Confronting them upon arrival was a city whose walls and houses had been reduced to a heap of rubble overgrown with weeds. The temple in whose splendor they had taken pride and received recognition was nothing more than rubbish and ashes. Furthermore, there was drought in the land, and economic depression seemed imminent. Despite the odds, the returnees had set their hearts towards rebuilding, and shortly after their arrival the foundation of the temple was laid (536 B.C.; Ezra 3:6–13). However, it seemed as though YAHWEH had once more turned His face against the nation. Through various misrepresentations to the Persian authorities, Judah's adversaries succeeded in bringing the work to a standstill, and it remained in that state for sixteen years (Ezra 4:1–5, 24). Discouraged, the repatriates became apathetic to spiritual priorities, indifferent to the needs of God's house, and content to worship in an unfinished structure. In this milieu, Haggai prophesied in order to awaken the lethargic community into resuming the work on the temple (Ezra 5:1–6:15). Meanwhile, the Persian Empire was experiencing tumultuous upheaval. Haggai's appeal to the people included an assurance that, despite the odds against it, God would guarantee the peace and prosperity of Jerusalem if the people would only be faithful to their responsibilities to Him. — W. A. Criswell et al., eds., *Believer's Study Bible, electronic ed*. (Nashville: Thomas Nelson, 1991), Hag 1:1.

2. **Let's think about Haggai the prophet. Who was he?**

   Haggai was a minor prophet and the writer of the book bearing his name (Hag. 1:1). Many think he was born in Israel before the 586 B.C. captivity and was taken to live in Babylon for the seventy years of captivity. King Cyrus, the Persian king, had issued a decree in 538 B.C. that allowed the Jews to return to their land and rebuild the temple. Haggai returned from Babylon with the remnant under Zerubbabel in 536 B.C., and the people began work on the temple (Ezra 4–6), but stopped shortly thereafter. The Samaritans hindered the work of the temple and wrote a letter to the Persian king, adding to the delay of the work. The remnant that returned found the land desolate, the crops failed, and hostility from their neighbors. They faced hard work, not to mention the enemies who attacked them.

In this context God called Haggai to preach to the people, encouraging them to complete the temple. Perhaps of all the prophets, Haggai and Zechariah might be considered the most successful prophets, because the temple was completed under their ministries.

Haggai preached his first message on September 1, 520 B.C. (Hag. 1:15). The prophet Zechariah, who also preached with him, began preaching between Haggai's second and third messages. The last message of Haggai was December 4, 518 B.C. The people responded and began work immediately on the temple, and completed it in four years, in 516 B.C. (Ezra 6:16). However, when the temple was rebuilt, it did not contain the ark of the covenant, so the Shekinah-glory cloud did not fill the Holy of Holies, nor were the Urim and Thummin present to supernaturally determine the will of God for the people. — Elmer Towns, *Bible Answers for Almost All Your Questions* (Nashville: Thomas Nelson, 2003).

3. Verse 1 dates the book. Put the date in our terms. What year is this?

All four oracles of Haggai are precisely dated in the year 520 B.C., the second year of the reign of Darius I (521–486 B.C.), king of Persia. The first oracle was delivered on the first day of Elul (August-September), the second on the twenty-first day of Tishri (September-October), and the last two on the twenty-fourth day of Kislev (November-December). Later the messages were compiled into what is now known as the Book of Haggai. For the historical background of the book, see Ezra 1–7. — W. A. Criswell et al., eds., *Believer's Study Bible, electronic ed.* (Nashville: Thomas Nelson, 1991), Hag 1:1.

4. **Verse 1. Here is one for the Bible scholars. Who was Zerubbabel?**

Consisting of only 1,131 words in thirty-eight verses in two chapters, Haggai is the second shortest book in the Old Testament. Haggai may not have been very effusive—but he was surely effective, for he was able to mobilize and motivate a mass of directionless people to resume the undertaking of a great project.

You see, approximately sixteen years earlier, they had been freed from captivity in Babylon. Led by their political leader, Zerubbabel, and Joshua, the high priest, these people of God had traveled several hundred miles back to Jerusalem and immediately set about doing what the Lord had commissioned them to do. They began to build the temple—the place where God's name could be praised, the place they could assemble to honor His name. They began to lay the foundation, but became intimidated by their enemies and divided by internal contention. So for sixteen years, the work sat idle. Weeds began to grow on the foundation as the people gave up on the project and instead turned to the construction of their own houses.

Throughout history, we see the power of the spoken word. In fact, historians tell us the single most important factor in England's preservation against Hitler's relentless attack was the oratorical ability of Winston Churchill. He was able to encourage and inspire a nation that would have otherwise gone under. Martin Luther King, Jr. was another one who was able to inspire hundreds of thousands of workers to march for civil rights by the power of his words. But neither of these men could hold a candle to Haggai because he spoke under the inspiration of the Spirit of God. — Jon Courson, *Jon Courson's Application Commentary: Volume Two: Psalms-Malachi* (Nashville, TN: Thomas Nelson, 2006), 885.

5. **What would you say is the main message of this short book for us?**

Maybe you were once excited about the things of God, excited about serving the Lord but have since grown weary by the squabbling of God's people or the attacks of the enemy. So you have decided to concentrate on your own life instead, tending to your own little world. This book is for you—for no matter how long it's been, we see in these pages that it's never too late to get going again. — Jon Courson, *Jon Courson's Application Commentary: Volume Two: Psalms-Malachi* (Nashville, TN: Thomas Nelson, 2006), 885–886.

6. Verses 2, 3. What is Haggai's essential message in these verses?

The Judeans have no stomach for construction work, and it seems doubtful that we would blame them. Their leaders, Zerubbabel and Joshua (1:1), may dwell in "paneled houses" (1:4), but most of the Judeans are desperately poor. Drought has led to crop failure (1:10–11), to hunger (1:6), and the encroachment of the desert into their farm lands. Inflation, always caused by shortages, eats holes in their purses (1:6). The enmity of Samaritan foreigners to the north and of quislings within the land several years earlier had discouraged them from any attempt at rebuilding their worship site (cf. Ezra 4:4–5). Why worry about the presence of God when reality is dictated by famine and fate and foreign power? After all, Persia rules the world and Judah is but its minor sub-province. Better to spend one's energies trying to stay alive than to bother with religious dreams! The harsh realities of life have to determine finally what one does in this world. — Elizabeth Rice Achtemeier, *Nahum–Malachi, Interpretation, a Bible Commentary for Teaching and Preaching* (Atlanta, GA: John Knox Press, 1986), 98.

7. Verse 9. They expected much but didn't get much. Why was this? What is the lesson for us?

The close of Yahweh's exhortation explicitly brings together the themes of the people's neglect of Yahweh's house while their own houses are in good shape, and their economic difficulties. You expected much. They had good reason to do that. Prophecies such as those in Isaiah 40–55 had encouraged them to do so. The sentence continues, but see, it turned out to be little. Their experience in the land was nowhere near as wonderful as one would have expected in light of such promises. Wherever people looked, there was disappointment. Haggai's explanation is the fact that they were preoccupied with what they could take to their own house (the word behind NIV home) at the expense of doing something about the state of Yahweh's house.

Thus the poor harvests were not "just one of those things." Like earlier prophets, Haggai sees the poor harvests as sent by Yahweh. Here for the first time Haggai utters terrible sentences of which Yahweh is the subject: I blew away ... I called for a drought. Of course it was implicit that Yahweh was behind the experiences described in verses 5–6, but only here does it become explicit. Yahweh acts in this way for reasons different from those that preoccupied those earlier prophets. Habakkuk and Zephaniah were appalled by the corruption that made it possible for clever and powerful people to do well at the expense of ordinary people, as well as by the inclination to turn to spiritual resources other than Yahweh. It was these wrongs that had caused Yahweh to send poor harvests in their day. Haggai apparently does not need to worry about such questions. It is the people's focus on their own houses rather than on Yahweh's that is the problem. Like other prophets, in this connection he needs to confront the people who take the lead in the people's political life and its worship life in order to get them to exercise their leadership. Further, he makes it clear that in this context Yahweh is not on the side of the poor. The whole community needs to focus on honoring Yahweh in the way symbolized by building the temple. — John Goldingay and Pamela J. Scalise, *Minor Prophets II, ed. W. Ward Gasque, Robert L. Hubbard Jr., and Robert K. Johnston, Understanding the Bible Commentary Series* (Grand Rapids, MI: Baker Books, 2012), 155–156.

8. What lesson did God want them to understand? What is the lesson for us?

'The LORD Almighty' wanted them to find the cause and the solution to their adversity; so he asked them, 'Why?' 'Why are you suffering? Why have your crops failed? Why do you put money in purses with holes in them?' The people had no doubt attributed their crop failure to natural causes: a freak drought, the poor quality of soil due to the seventy years of neglect. God wanted them to understand that it was his doing, not a chance happening or a twist of fate, but a divine judgement. Fruitfulness or sterility come from God, not from nature. — Tim Shenton, *Haggai: An Expositional Commentary, Exploring the Bible Commentary* (Leominster, UK: Day One, 2007), 34.

9. Verse 14. How did the people respond to Haggai's message?

From time to time the preaching of the Word of God strikes home, and a life is genuinely changed. When that happens in large numbers, you have a revival.

This happened under Haggai's preaching. We recall from our study of the earlier prophets that the warnings given to the Jewish people before God's judgment by the Assyrian and Babylonian invasions generally went unheeded. Micah had some success. But for the most part the people could not have cared less about the prophets' warnings. To our joy we see a different kind of response from the people of Judah under Haggai's ministry. They had been negligent of God's work. They had invented flimsy excuses as to why they were inactive. But they were not basically hostile to God or his commandments, as the people living before the exile had been. They really wanted to please God. So when the word of the Lord came to them by Haggai, they recognized it as a true word of God and did what God commanded.

The chapter concludes: "So the LORD stirred up the spirit of Zerubbabel son of Shealtiel, governor of Judah, and the spirit of Joshua son of Jehozadak, the high priest, and the spirit of the whole remnant of the people. They came and began to work on the house of the LORD Almighty, their God, on the twenty-fourth day of the sixth month in the second year of King Darius" (vv. 14–15). — James Montgomery Boice, *Come to the Waters: Daily Bible Devotions for Spiritual* Refreshment (Grand Rapids, MI: Baker, 2011).

10. Verse 15. Major changes were in store. How long did it take those changes to take place?

There is an interesting note in that last verse, where we are told that the people resumed the work on the twenty-fourth day of the month. If we compare that with the first verse of the chapter, where we are told that Haggai began to preach on the first day of the month, we find that the change came about in just twenty-three days. Haggai spoke on August 30, 520 BC. The work began on the twenty-first of September.

I wonder if there is a date like that in your life or if today might possibly become that day. I do not mean the day of your conversion; you may or may not have a known day for that. I mean the day in which you finally got the priorities of your life straightened out and determined that from that time on you would put God and his work first in everything. You need to do that. You need to ask yourself these questions: Is my own comfort of greater importance to me than the work of God? Am I making increasing efforts to get ahead financially but finding greater and greater disappointment in my life? If the answer is yes, just turn around and get on with God's business. Obey him. Put him first in your life.[161] — James Montgomery Boice, *Come to the Waters: Daily Bible Devotions for Spiritual Refreshment* (Grand Rapids, MI: Baker, 2011).

11. Haggai 2.1. How much time between chapters 1 and 2?

It was nearly a month after work started when Haggai was given a new word from the Lord. We can guess that during the intervening weeks efforts were concentrated on clearing the site of rubble, redressing stone that was fit for use, testing for safety the walls that still remained (for we know that even after bombing a surprising amount of a stone building may remain standing), and organizing teams of workmen for their particular tasks. Such preparations on a sixty-year-old ruin, without any mechanical aids, would tax the endurance of even the most enthusiastic; hence the need of encouragement. But there was another factor. — Joyce G.

Baldwin, *Haggai, Zechariah and Malachi: An Introduction and Commentary, vol. 28, Tyndale Old Testament Commentaries* (Downers Grove, IL: InterVarsity Press, 1972), 49.

12. Haggai 2.3. How did this new temple compare with the old temple?

The revered elders who remembered the temple before its destruction must often have spoken nostalgically of its splendour. Some of them no doubt took part in the abortive attempt to rebuild in 538 BC (Ezra 3:8–13). Past disappointment was making them gloomy about the present and future. The new temple would never be like the old; they had no resources to pay skilled craftsmen from abroad, as Solomon had done, and they could not begin to think of covering the interior with gold (1 Kgs 6:21, 22). In spite of the work they had already put in there was nothing to show for it. Unfavourable comparison between the present and the past undermined all incentive to persevere. — Joyce G. Baldwin, *Haggai, Zechariah and Malachi: An Introduction and Commentary, vol. 28, Tyndale Old Testament Commentaries* (Downers Grove, IL: InterVarsity Press, 1972), 50.

13. Why wasn't this temple as nice as the old?

They had none of the wealth that had gone into King Solomon's temple. When the first temple had been built there was an abundance of material waiting to be used. Although King David had been forbidden by God to build a temple himself, he had not been idle. He had spent much time gathering together fabric for the building. And then, remember that King Solomon himself was also a wealthy man. He had many mines which yielded precious metals and he had much money with which to buy timber from Lebanon. What had Zerubbabel got as he started on the rebuilding work? Hardly anything!

Not only were the Jews of 520 B.C. poorly off for materials, they also lacked the craftsmen who had the necessary skills to perform such a tremendous task as rebuilding the temple for God's glory. What had happened to all the Jewish craftsmen? Many of them had perished during the years of exile in Babylon. Perhaps some of the trades had died out altogether and many of the skills had been lost through lack of use.

The Jews became discouraged further when they considered God's plans for the rebuilt temple. What had the prophets said? They had spoken of a future temple which would be far more glorious than Solomon's temple. Isaiah and Jeremiah had prophesied of a marvellous house of God (e.g. Isaiah 60) and Ezekiel had even described it in great detail (Ezekiel 40–43). No wonder the people became discouraged when they realized that their efforts were puny and the end result would be far, far inferior to Solomon's temple. — Michael Bentley, *Building for God's Glory: Haggai and Zechariah Simply Explained, Welwyn Commentary Series* (Darlington, England: Evangelical Press, 1989), 53–54.

14. Verse 4. What exactly does it mean to be strong?

Be strong!
We are not here to play, to dream, to drift:
We have hard work to do and loads to lift;
Shun not the struggle: face it 'tis God's gift.

Be strong!
Say not the days are evil who's to blame?
And fold the hands and acquiesce O shame!
Stand up, speak out, and bravely, in God's Name,

Be strong!
It matters not how deep entrenched the wrong,
How hard the battle goes, the day, how long;
Faint not, fight on! Tomorrow comes the song.

—Maltbie Babcock (d. 1901) / *Galaxie Software, 10,000 Sermon Illustrations* (Biblical Studies Press, 2002).

15. YBH. Yes, but how? How do we be strong?

Ephesians 6:10 introduces the first prong of this battle plan: Our only true resource in the struggle against the powers of darkness is the Lord's power. "Be strong in the Lord and in the strength of His might."

The Greek verb translated "be strong" (endunousthe) is a present passive imperative. This means the strength comes from God (passive voice); it is to be a continual, habitual part of the believer's experience (present tense); and it is absolutely necessary if victory is to be realized (imperative mood). Ephesians 6 uses three words for power (empowered, strength, might), which highlights the truth that every child of God has accessibility to divine power.

As 1 John 4:4 states, "Greater is He who is in you than he who is in the world." Second Chronicles 20:15 reminds us, "The battle is not yours but God's." Our Commander in Chief has won the war. Christ defeated the enemy at the cross. We fight a defeated foe. Power comes from the Lord, not our own ingenuity or methods. Of course, we are not inactive. Scripture commands us to stand and resist the enemy. We should give maximum effort to follow the Lord's commands and put on the full armor He provides.

A friend of mine visited a Navy Seal installation in California, and he saw a large plaque that says, "The enemy thanks you for not giving 100 percent today." Our enemy is pleased when we fail to give 100 percent, but he is also pleased if we give 100 percent and rely only on our own strength. God uses our efforts, but they are insufficient. We must be strong in Him.

S. Lewis Johnson says, "You notice the Apostle does not say, 'be strong in human plans.' He does not say, 'be strong in human methods.' He does not say, 'be strong in the latest ideas that sweep over the evangelical church, but 'be strong in the Lord and the power of His might.' " We need the Lord. We don't need Him and something else. We need Him. — Mark Hitchcock, *101 Answers to Questions about Satan, Demons, and Spiritual Warfare* (Eugene, OR: Harvest House, 2014).

16. Why is it important that we "be strong"?

Our son Zach is a strength and conditioning performance coach at a division one university. For their engagement photo, Zach and his fiancée, Caleigh, chose a word that represents their goal for their future: strength. Their wise choice impressed us. It's a great goal for all of us to live a strong life—emotionally, physically, relationally, and spiritually. We know it is God's goal for each of us because Psalm 27:14 states it plainly: "Be strong and take heart and wait for the LORD."

But how can we partner with God to gain a strong life?

- "Be strong and very courageous. Be careful to obey all the law my servant Moses gave you; do not turn from it to the right or to the left, that you may be successful wherever you go" (Joshua 1:7)—Fully obey God's Word.

- "I long to see you so that I may impart to you some spiritual gift to make you strong—that is, that you and I may be mutually encouraged by each other's faith" (Romans 1:11-12)—Use your gifts to encourage others and let others encourage you.

- "Be on your guard; stand firm in the faith; be courageous; be strong. Do everything in love" (1 Corinthians 16:13-14)—Be vigilant, stand firm in your core beliefs, and do it in love.

- "Finally, be strong in the Lord and in his mighty power. Put on the full armor of God, so that you can take your stand against the devil's schemes" (Ephesians 6:10-11)—Wear God's armor (which is the Word).

- "You then, my son, be strong in the grace that is in Christ Jesus. And the things you have heard me say" (2 Timothy 2:1-2)—Obey the Word you have heard.

- "I write to you, young men, because you are strong, and the word of God lives in you" (1 John 2:14)—Let God's Word live in you.

Our son Zach was named Ohio's strongest man because of his weight-lifting ability. In a spiritual sense, this world needs more couples who can carry their own weight, help carry the weight of the world, and carry the weight of those who are broken and too weak to carry their own weight. In Becoming a Woman of Influence, I share a prayer I prayed for myself, our marriage, and our family: "Lord, let us be like an aircraft carrier. Help our lives be so strong that others can land, get refueled, and restocked. Then let them take off to the mission You have called them to."

Make it your goal to do some spiritual circuit training every day. Pray, read your Bible, memorize Scripture, praise God for His goodness, and share the Good News with others. Your marriage will be stronger, your children will be stronger, and the influence you leave for those around you in your workplace, church, and community will be stronger too. Pump some iron for Jesus! — Bill Farrel and Pam Farrel, *A Couple's Journey with God* (Eugene, OR: Harvest House, 2012).

17. Verse 9. What does he mean that the glory of this temple will be greater than the glory of the last temple?

When they realized that the work of their hands was far inferior to the temple that was built by Solomon, the repatriates became pessimistic about their efforts. Haggai assures them that "the glory of this latter temple shall be greater than the former" (v. 9) because "the Desire of All Nations" shall come to it (v. 7). The latter phrase may mean that all which is desirable and valuable among the nations shall be brought into the temple (cf. Is. 60:5, 11). Some have estimated that the gold inlay alone in Solomon's temple was worth over $20,000,000. There is no question that the Lord could bring in the precious metals and stones (v. 8; cf. Ps. 50:12), but Haggai's message means more than that. Jewish tradition and early Christian literature identify "the Desire of All Nations" as the Messiah. Although Zerubbabel's temple was probably leveled to the foundations during Herod's renovation, a continuity exists between the two so that they are both designated as the second temple. Jesus Christ, who is God incarnate, set foot on Herod's temple; and witnesses saw and experienced God's glory in Him (John 1:14–18). The promised peace was effected at Calvary (Col. 1:20), is experienced by the Christian (Rom. 5:1; Phil. 4:7), and is ultimately found only in the Person of the Prince of Peace (Is. 9:6, 7). — W. A. Criswell et al., eds., *Believer's Study Bible, electronic ed.* (Nashville: Thomas Nelson, 1991), Hag 2:7.

18. Haggai 2.10 – 14. Someone explain this teaching.

Haggai was to pose two questions to the priests. "If a piece of meat that has been offered to the Lord accidentally touches some other object, does the object it touches become holy?"

"No," the priests answered.

Second, "If someone is ceremonially unclean because he touched a dead body, can he make others ceremonially unclean by touching them?"

"Yes," the priests answered.

Simply put, holiness cannot be passed on—but corruption and pollution can be. In other words, if you hang around sin, you can't help but be affected. But simply hanging around a church doesn't make you a Christian. You've got to be obedient to the Lord personally. — Jon Courson, *Jon Courson's Application Commentary: Volume Two: Psalms-Malachi* (Nashville, TN: Thomas Nelson, 2006), 888.

19. Summary. What is the lesson of the book of Haggai?

The focus of Haggai is the "unfinished temple." The people had begun rebuilding the temple, but had stopped. The prophet reminded them that, "the glory of this latter house shall be greater than of the former" (Hag. 2:9 KJV). By that he meant that the former house, Solomon's temple, had contained the Shekinah-glory cloud, but the house that they were building, Zerubbabel's temple, would experience a far greater glory when the Lord Jesus Christ visited it during His earthly ministry. — Elmer Towns, *Bible Answers for Almost All Your Questions* (Nashville: Thomas Nelson, 2003).

20. **What do you want to recall from today's conversation?**

21. **How can we support one another in prayer this week?**

7 Minor Prophets, Lesson #10

Good Questions Have Small Groups Talking

www.joshhunt.com

Again, I'd email your group and ask them to do a little background reading. It is almost impossible to get fully up to speed on a passage like this with a little background reading. They don't need to do a lot of reading. Half an hour or so reading the notes in a study Bible will make the conversation a whole lot more interesting. Alternatively, you might email just a few of your readers and ask them to give a brief report on some of the background info.

Malachi 1

OPEN

Let's each share your name and one thing you are grateful for.

DIG

1. **Overview. What do we know about Malachi?**

   As with Joel, we don't know very much about Malachi personally. But we do know his name means "Messenger" and, in a sense, that is all we need to know for it's not the messenger but the message that matters. It's the message that makes the difference.

If you heard a knock on your door and opened it to find a FedEx driver standing there with an envelope in his hand addressed to you, you wouldn't ask him about his ancestors, his favorite foods, or his political leanings. Your interests would lie with the message he carried for you. The enemy, however, comes to each of us and whispers, "Who do you think you are, witnessing? Who do you think you are to be teaching or serving?" The enemy's tactic is to condemn us constantly in an effort to neutralize us (Revelation 12:10). But we must realize that it's the message with which we've been entrusted that matters. Therefore, be faithful in what the Lord has given you to do. Pass on what He's entrusted to you. Don't get sucked into the lie that, because you're not spiritual enough, you can't do or say anything on behalf of the Lord. — Jon Courson, *Jon Courson's Application Commentary: Volume Two: Psalms-Malachi* (Nashville, TN: Thomas Nelson, 2006), 920–921.

2. Malachi is the last book in the Old Testament. Where does it fit in the chronology of the Bible?

Written in about 400 B.C., the Book of Malachi brings down the curtain on the Old Testament. And as the curtain comes down, the voice of God rings out. Of the fifty-five verses that comprise this book, forty-seven are spoken by God directly. That's a higher percentage than that of any other book in the Bible. Truly, God's voice penetrates and resounds through the book before us.

Malachi is the only prophet to end his prophecy with a warning. Other prophets ended on a note of hope. But in Malachi, the Old Testament closes with a warning because it's setting the stage for the blessing, the redemptive work of Christ Jesus as seen in the first book of the New Testament—the Gospel of Matthew.

It had been a hundred years since Zechariah and Haggai had been on the scene encouraging the people of Judah to finish the work of reconstructing the temple that had been destroyed by the Babylonians in 586 B.C. Zechariah and Haggai encouraged the people to return to work—and the people responded. The temple was rebuilt; the walls were restored. Yet success had its own dangers because, after the temple was rebuilt and the walls restored, the people began to kick back a bit. And as they did, their cutting edge was lost. They began to lose their fire and passion. Oh, they weren't committing big, blatant sins. But a mediocrity had crept into them. So the Lord sent Malachi to speak to His people concerning the lukewarm state of their hearts. — Jon Courson, *Jon Courson's Application Commentary: Volume Two: Psalms-Malachi* (Nashville, TN: Thomas Nelson, 2006), 920.

3. What is the situation in Israel during Malachi's day?

WE DO NOT KNOW MUCH about Malachi. He served in the postexilic period, later than the early years when the greatest crises took place. By his day, both the wall and the temple had been rebuilt. Nehemiah, Zerubbabel, and Joshua were names in the past. The returned remnant had settled down. Nothing of great significance had occurred very recently. There was no spectacular restoration of the glory of God to the temple, envisaged by Ezekiel (43:4). The ritual was carried out, but without fervor or enthusiasm.

This is the situation Malachi addresses. It makes his words peculiarly appropriate for believers living in similar days of lethargy. There is not much going on: the political situation is stable, religious freedom is secure, the prescribed rituals are carried out—but all of it lacks not only passion but integrity, life-transformation, zeal, honor in relationships and promises, the fear of the Lord. The returned Jews are characterized by a world-weary cynicism that will not be moved. — D. A. Carson, *For the Love of God: A Daily Companion for Discovering the Riches of God's Word., vol.* 2 (Wheaton, IL: Crossway Books, 1998), 25.

4. **Verse 1 begins with "a prophecy" (NIV2011) or "an oracle" (NIV84). How does your translation have it?**

Malachi introduced his book with the familiar prophetic designation, an oracle (NIV, NASB, NRSV) or "burden" (KJV, NKJV). "Burden" would suggest the idea of a heavy message—one containing stern warnings or judgment. Malachi's prophecy does indeed contain a severe rebuke for his fellow countrymen who were engaged in sinful practices. (For a further discussion of the word oracle, see the "Deeper Discoveries" section for Nahum 1.)

From the outset the prophet made clear that his message was not just personal opinion but the word of the Lord. We should always keep in mind as we study the Bible that this is no ordinary book; it is God's word to the human race. The phrase, an oracle: the word of the Lord, is used exclusively after the Babylonian exile and occurs elsewhere only in Zechariah 9:1 and 12:1 (exact wording in Hebrew text).

Malachi apparently preached his message orally to the people of Israel, possibly during a festal gathering. Without question, the setting was in the postexilic period, although scholars debate the specific time of Malachi's ministry. The flagrant disrespect for God's worship and other conditions described in the book could never have occurred while Nehemiah was present in Jerusalem. Either Nehemiah had not yet arrived, or more likely, Malachi delivered these sermons between Nehemiah's two terms as governor (about 433 B.C.). — *Holman Old Testament Commentary – Nahum-Malachi.*

5. **Verse 2 begins with a declaration of God's love for them. Why might they have been tempted to believe that God did not love them?**

During the postexilic period, the nation experienced economic hardships and chafed under the rule of foreign domination. A century after the first return to the land under Zerubbabel, Israel was still just a tiny, struggling country on the outskirts of the vast Persian Empire. Clearly, many people had become discouraged because of the economic difficulties and other hardships. They even questioned whether God loved them. However, they were a sinful people, and Malachi pointed out in his book that one reason for their difficulties (even some of their economic woes) was unfaithfulness to the Lord. — *Holman Old Testament Commentary – Nahum-Malachi.*

6. What does it mean that God hated Esau?

The second evidence of God's love that Malachi presented was God's electing grace (Mal. 2b-3). As the firstborn in the family, Esau should have inherited both the blessing and the birthright, but the Lord gave them to his younger brother Jacob (Gen. 25:21-23). The descendants of Esau had their land assigned to them, but God gave the Edomites no covenants of blessing as He did to Jacob's descendants.

The statement that God loved Jacob but hated Esau has troubled some people. Paul quoted it in Romans 9:10-13 to prove God's electing grace for both Israel and all who trust Jesus Christ for salvation. But the verb "hate" must not be defined as a positive expression of the wrath of God. God's love for Jacob was so great that, in comparison, His actions toward Esau looked like hatred. As an illustration, Jacob loved Rachel so much that his relationship to Leah seemed like hatred (Gen. 29:20, 30-31; see also Deut. 21:15-17). When Jesus called His disciples to "hate" their own family (Luke 14:26), He was using the word "hate" in a similar way. Our love for Christ may occasionally move us to do things that appear like hatred to those whom we love (see Matt. 12:46-50).

Someone said to Dr. Arno C. Gaebelein, the gifted Hebrew Christian leader of a generation ago, "I have a serious problem with Malachi 1:3, where God says, 'Esau I have hated.'" Dr. Gaebelein replied, "I have a greater problem with Malachi 1:2, where God says, 'Jacob, I have loved.'" We certainly can't explain the love and grace of God, nor do we have to, but we can experience God's grace and love as trust Christ and walk with Him. The Lord is even willing to be "the God of Jacob." — *Old Testament - The Bible Exposition Commentary – The Prophets.*

7. Does God hate?

"Hate" is a powerful word. We are taught from childhood to avoid hatred at all costs and to obey the command of Christ to love everyone, including our enemies. So it's shocking to read the words of Malachi, who declared that God loved Jacob but hated Esau (Mal. 1:2–3). How can a God of love hate?

Let's begin by examining the Hebrew terms. The Old Testament uses two words that can be translated "hate": sane (sah-NAY) and ma'as (ma-AS); they differ only slightly in meaning. In fact, Old Testament writers sometimes used them interchangeably. For example, the prophet Amos placed them side-by-side to express God's disgust with Israelite worship, saying, "I hate, I despise your religious feasts; I cannot stand your assemblies" (Amos 5:21 NIV, emphasis mine).

While sane and ma'as can express intense emotional displeasure toward something, "hating" in ancient Near East cultures has more to do with one's priorities than with his or her emotions. For example, Esau "despised" his birthright when he made a freewill choice for a bowl of soup over his covenant blessing (Gen. 25:29–34). Esau didn't have intense negative emotions about his birthright—he certainly didn't "hate" it as we would use the term; in fact, he fought hard to regain what he had lost and was inconsolable when he failed.

In another example, Genesis 29 tells the story of Jacob's two wives and how he "loved" Rachel and "hated" her sister, Leah. Again, the term indicates Jacob's choice to favor one over the other. He wasn't repulsed by Leah. After all, he did conceive at least seven children with her!

Furthermore, in the New Testament, Jesus required His followers to "hate" their money, their families, and even their own lives (Matt. 6:24; Luke 14:26; John 12:25). Obviously, He wasn't instructing His disciples to treat others cruelly. The issue at hand was priority, choosing discipleship over all other things and choosing Christ over all other relationships.

It would be convenient to stop here and pretend the uglier side of "hate" didn't exist; however, we cannot ignore the only other significant use of "hate" in the Old Testament. In Genesis 37, "hate" describes the obsessive loathing of Joseph's older brothers. They plotted to kill him, but when a caravan of slave traders happened to pass by, they decided to sell him off instead. Clearly the term "hate" can describe either meaning, dispassionate choice or passionate loathing. So where does that leave us with Malachi 1:2–3?

The book of Malachi was a warning to that nation of Judah, who profaned the temple by offering substandard sacrifices and keeping the best livestock for themselves. He accused the priests of "despising" their covenant blessing, much like Esau "despised" his birthright. By recalling the story of Jacob (whose name was changed to Israel) and Esau (whose descendants formed the nation of Edom), the prophet drew a clear parallel:

Jacob prized the covenant.	Esau despised the covenant.
God promised to rescue Israel (Deut. 4:29–31; 30:1–10).	God vowed to condemn Edom (Jer. 49:7–22; Ezek. 35).

By the time of Malachi, both prophecies had been fulfilled. God had restored a faithful remnant of Israel to the Promised Land; however, they could not afford to become smug. By despising their covenant blessing, the Israelites ran the risk of suffering Esau's fate. In other words, "Take heed, Israel. Esau despised his birthright and Edom incurred the judicial abandonment of God. What do you think will happen if you despise your birthright?"

God's "hatred" is a double-edged sword. While it is indeed filled with emotion, it is not motivated by it. Like His wrath, His act of choosing one over another ("hating") is absolutely righteous and utterly just. — Charles R. Swindoll, *Insights on Romans, Swindoll's New Testament Insights* (Grand Rapids, MI: Zondervan, 2010), 193–194.

8. Do you see yourself as loved by God?

Two times during the ministry of Jesus, the windows of heaven opened up and the Father spoke audibly to Jesus and everyone around him, saying, "This is my Son, whom I love" (Matthew 3:17; 17:5). Apparently God, in his infinite wisdom, knew that from time to time Jesus needed to be reassured and reminded of his Father's love. Every now and then, Jesus needed to hear his Father say, "You are my beloved Son" (Mark 1:11b, TLB). I suspect the people you teach need to be reminded as well.

Interestingly enough, Paul uses the same Greek root to describe God's attitude toward us. In 1 Thessalonians 1:4, Paul states that all Christians are "loved by God." We are, quite simply, God's beloved. God's love for us is one of the basic truths of the gospel. It is one of the first things we teach our children in Sunday school. Children who don't know very much about God still sing, "Jesus loves me, this I know, for the Bible tells me so." God's love for us offers a common theme in our songs and in our sermons.

Unfortunately, many Christians don't feel all that loved by God. They don't see themselves as God's beloved. They feel as though God is either disappointed in them or has forgotten about them altogether. They may believe on some detached, intellectual level that God loves them, but they don't feel it in their hearts. If we want to create disciples, we will constantly remind people that they are the beloved of God.

We are often awed by impressive people, but we generally love only those people whom we feel love us. I might be impressed by movie stars, athletes, or business people, but I usu-ally don't come to love those people unless I have personal contact with them and sense that they care for me. In the same way, we can be impressed with God whether or not we feel that he loves us. But we will only love God to the degree that we are convinced that he loves us. We will only live as God's beloved to the degree that we feel loved by God.

Our hymn books often contain various love songs to God, but God also has love songs written to us. Zephaniah 3:17 states: "The Lord your God is with you, he is mighty to save. He will take great delight in you, he will quiet you with his love, he will rejoice over you with singing." Imagine! The God of the entire universe who created the stars with the command of his resonant voice rejoices over you with singing! The God of the entire universe loves you and takes delight in you. If that doesn't cause you to smile, you may want to check your pulse.

Do you see yourself as someone who is beloved by God? Better yet, do you feel that you are the apple of your Father's eye? Do the people you teach feel that they are God's beloved? If not, I invite you to pray right now and tell God you want to exchange whatever belief you have about yourself for the truth that you are the beloved of God. Then I would encourage you to lead your class to do the same. Until their self-image is one of being loved by God, they will never behave as children of God. — Josh Hunt, *Disciplemaking Teachers*, 1996.

9. What advice would you have for a friend who said he didn't feel loved by God?

Father, your love never ceases. Never. Though we spurn you, ignore you, disobey you, you will not change. Our evil cannot diminish your love. Our goodness cannot increase it. Our faith does not earn it anymore than our stupidity jeopardizes it. You don't love us less if we fail. You don't love us more if we succeed.

Your love never ceases. — Max Lucado, *Everyday Blessings: Inspirational Thoughts from the Published Works of Max Lucado.* (Nashville, TN: Thomas Nelson, Inc., 2004).

10. What name for God is used in verse 4? How does your translation have it?

Note that the name God uses in Malachi 1:4 is "Lord of hosts" ("Lord Almighty" in the niv), that is, "the Lord of the armies," a name used 24 times in Malachi and nearly 300 times in the

Old Testament. This is the "military" name of God, for "hosts" comes from a Hebrew word which means "to wage war." The Lord is the Commander of the hosts and heaven: the stars (Isa. 40:26; Gen. 2:1), the angels (Ps. 103:20-21), the armies of Israel (Ex. 12:41), and all who trust in Him (Ps. 46:7, 11). — *Old Testament - The Bible Exposition Commentary – The Prophets.*

11. What does it tell us about God that He is the Lord of armies?

El Shaddai is the Hebrew word that we translate "God Almighty." This phrase has been given several meanings by scholars: "the All-Sufficient One", "the Thundered," "the Mountain-Like One", "the Overpowerer." All of these word pictures point to the same conception: God is the All-Powerful, the All-Ruler, which in Greek is the word Pantocrator. One of the most important names the early church gave to Jesus was Pantocrator, All-Powerful All-Ruler.

God revealed his name as Almighty to the patriarchs because he was making promises to them. They could trust him because he is all-powerful. God explains in Exodus 6 that the name Yahweh is associated with faithfulness, because at that time God was going to fulfill his promises to the patriarchs. Moses could trust God because he is faithful. In the kingdom period, the name Adonai came to prominence, to remind Israel of their real Lord and King. In and after their exile, when Israel was small and ruled by mighty empires, God brought into focus the name Lord of Hosts (Adonai Sabaoth, which the NIV renders "Lord Almighty"), to remind them that God's army is the mightiest of all.

As we approach God in worship, we should remember that he is Almighty and tremble before him. The fear of God is the beginning of wisdom, and thus also of worship. When Job cried out to God, God revealed his power, and Job found great comfort in the Almighty (Job 38–42). When we see people rise up against God and try to warp his design for society and destroy his church, we should join in God's laughter, because the Almighty holds them in derision

(Psalm 2). Thus, God's power places in us a holy fear, a great comfort, and finally laughter and joy.

The new name God gives in the gospel is Jesus, the Savior. And what a Savior he is. He is the faithful, almighty, promise-keeping Yahweh. He is the Master who rules all. He is the Lord of Armies. — R.C. Sproul, *Before the Face of God: Book 4: A Daily Guide for Living from Ephesians, Hebrews, and James, electronic ed.* (Grand Rapids: Baker Book House; Ligonier Ministries, 1994), 244–245.

12. Verse 6ff (especially verse 8). What complaint does God have against the people? What is the application for us?

In Malachi 1:6 God tells the people of Israel that he has an offense against them. Their minds race as they try to figure out what they've done wrong; finally, they ask for some clarification: "Well, what did we do?"

Speaking on God's behalf, the prophet Malachi responds, "What did you do? You know the laws about making sacrifices. You know that you ought to go out into your herds and select the best, most valuable, most prized lamb from your flock for your offering to God. But instead of doing what you know to do, you are heading out to your fields and intentionally overlooking the top sheep in the herd. Rather than selecting your prized lamb, you look for one that's sick and blind and lame and leaning against the fence, ready to keel over! You grab that one and race for the altar before it dies, thinking, 'It'll suffice. It's only for God.' "

Malachi then said to the people, "This is what God says. 'Don't even bother building a fire. Don't waste your time. I don't want the sick and lame and blind and almost-dead lamb. What a mockery to me! Either bring me the prized lamb or bring me nothing at all!' "

Can you imagine receiving a rebuke like that directly from God? I read the passage that afternoon all those years ago and felt as though something had permanently shifted inside of me. The Spirit of God seemed to be saying to me that everything I do in Christian leadership—every plan I put together, every meeting I lead, every talk I give—needs to be my best lamb, my very best offering! Not so that I'll operate out of paranoia or wild perfectionism, but so that I'll live from my heart's deep desire to honor God.

In my thirty-plus years as a senior pastor, nobody has ever set a standard for me to try to reach with regard to my preaching. It would be a waste of their time, because my internal standard will always be higher than that which others can mandate. People at Willow have had to tolerate a lot of pretty sorry sermons, but at those particular times in my life, those talks were the best ones I could give.

I wonder what would happen to every church on the planet if every pastor, staff member, volunteer, elder or deacon, and servant in children's ministry were to say, "You don't have to worry about me. I'm committed to giving my best lamb, every single day. I'm going to live in vital union with God, and I'm going to consistently render my most excellent offering. The standard I have established is higher than any you could possibly set for me!"

What would happen to our leadership? What would happen to our preaching? What would happen to our music? What would happen to our administrative functions if everybody in the church established their own level of quality control based on the excellence of Jesus Christ and remained dogged in their determination to honor him with their best every time?

We must fight for excellence because it is excellence that honors God. It is excellence that inspires people. And it is excellence that means trouble for the enemy of our souls.
— Bill Hybels, *Axiom: Powerful Leadership Proverbs* (Grand Rapids, MI: Zondervan, 2008).

13. We don't offer blind or lame animals. What do we do that offends God?

Occasionally I'll hear someone claim that the people of the Old Testament had to give under compulsion, while those in New Testament times are somehow more "free" to give. But that comparison is false, for we are just as responsible to tithe as those living in Old Testament times. The fact is, the people living in Malachi's time were supposed to be giving as an expression of their love for God, and their tithe was to reflect that spirit. If they failed to give out of love, it revealed a lack of spiritual vitality.

For example, in Malachi 1:8 we read, "When you offer the blind as a sacrifice, is it not evil? And when you offer the lame and sick, is it not evil? Offer it then to your governor! Would he be pleased with you? Would he accept you favorably?" You see, the Jews were supposed to bring a healthy animal and offer it as a sacrifice to the Lord. But some people were looking around for their smallest, weakest animal, or they were offering God a sick or blind animal. They were giving God their leftovers, and it revealed a weak spirituality. So Malachi asks them, "Would you give that to the government?" Try handing the tax man a smaller portion than he deserves and see what it gets you! The government wants what it is due, and won't settle for something else.

The Lord is the same way. That's why Malachi says, "Cursed be the deceiver who has in his flock a male, and takes a vow, but sacrifices to the Lord what is blemished" (1:14). A person should not come to God and offer Him the scraps. If we recognize God as King and Lord, we ought to be unwilling to give Him leftovers. He demands what is best. We are to be committed to excellence in everything we do. He expects the best we have to offer, whether that is with our money, our worship services, or anything else we do in His name. I don't believe God is pleased with anyone who eschews excellence to offer Him something unprepared and unsacrificial.

In the Old Testament, the people brought their offerings to God and made it a matter of priority. As we come to Him, we are to do the same. That means we don't give God the change left over after we've bought everything we want, nor do we offer Him the time we have left after packing our schedules with our own motivations and ambitions. God doesn't seek the talents we have left over after all our efforts have been put toward our own selfish ends, nor does He desire a tip out of the income He has entrusted to our care. Tithing has always been a matter of priority to God, and it should still be a matter of priority in our own lives. — David Jeremiah, *Giving to God: Study Guide* (Nashville, TN: Thomas Nelson Publishers, 2001), 25–26.

14. What do we learn about worship from this passage?

A number of words in the Bible are translated "worship." The one used the most often means "to bow down and do homage." Another biblical word for worship means "to kiss toward." Put the two words together, and you will have a good idea of what real worship is.

We worship God because He is worthy, bowing down in reverence and respect before Him. But we also "kiss toward" Him, which speaks of tenderness and intimacy.

We ought to be learning all we can about worship, because it will be one of the primary activities of heaven. And Jesus made it clear that there is a right and a wrong way to worship. There is true and false worship.

The Pharisees, who considered themselves the worship gurus of their day, missed the target by a mile. Jesus said of them, "'These people draw near to Me with their mouth, and honor Me with their lips, but their heart is far from Me. And in vain they worship Me, teaching as doctrines the commandments of men'" (Matthew 15:8-9).

Some people are too flippant and casual with God. They seem to think of Him as their celestial Big Buddy and approach Him that way in prayer: "Hey, Lord, how are You doing?" We need to be careful about that. In the Old Testament, God once said to a group of distracted and careless worshipers: "'A son honors his father, and a servant his master. If I am a father, where is the honor due me? If I am a master, where is the respect due me?' says the Lord Almighty" (Malachi 1:6, NIV).

Still others may recognize God as holy and all-powerful and may even tremble before Him, but they don't realize that God wants to be known in an intimate and personal way.

Yes, we are to revere and honor God. But we're also to embrace Him in closeness. We are to engage our hearts, with no hypocrisy. And that's where true worship begins. — Greg Laurie, *Daily Hope for Hurting Hearts: A Devotional* (Dana Point, CA: Kerygma Publishing—Allen David Books, 2011).

15. The animals are going to be killed anyway. Why not bring the lame ones?

When you give God your firstfruits, you not only give Him the first, you give Him the best. In Malachi 1, the Israelites brought God the worst of their leftovers for their sacrifices—the sick, blind, and lame animals. Sometimes that's what we bring God—our leftover time, energy, and devotion. We come to God when we're not at our peak.

The story of Cain and Abel in the Scripture above serves as a reminder that God isn't pleased with those who do not offer firstfruits.

Cain killed his brother over this very matter. Abel brought God the best because he believed God desired and deserved the best. Cain's offering showed that he thought God deserved something but not necessarily the best.

If we're not worshipping God by bringing Him our firstfruits, we're likely giving our firstfruits to something else. To find out where your firstfruits are going, ask yourself, "What gets my best time and my undivided attention?"

Whenever you give God what is first in your heart, time, and treasure, you're honoring Him as God.

How can you honor God with your firstfruits today? — Tony Evans, *A Moment for Your Soul: Devotions to Lift You up* (Eugene, OR: Harvest House, 2012).

16. Verse 10. Why does God not accept their offerings?

This verse adds yet another catastrophic result of the priests' irreverence. Here the Lord tells them that their worship is worthless in his eyes. He even calls for them to shut the doors of the temple! No worship is better than irreverent worship!

We cannot read the Lord's words here without thinking of the similar message delivered by the Lord Jesus to the church of Laodicea: 'I know your works, that you are neither cold nor hot. I could wish you were cold or hot. So then, because you are lukewarm, and neither cold nor hot, I will spew you out of my mouth' (Rev. 3:15–16).

This must not be used as an excuse not to worship. God commands both that we worship him and that we worship him in the right way. And the right way is, of course, that which the Lord Jesus indicated in his conversation with the Samaritan woman: 'God is Spirit, and those who worship him must worship in spirit and truth' (John 4:24).

To worship God in spirit is to worship him with our spirits engaged. It is to worship with our hearts going out after God.

To worship him in truth is to do so according to what he himself has revealed. It is to worship according to the truth of his Word. We are not to include anything in worship that is not clearly sanctioned or warranted by the Word of God, no matter how it attracts crowds and pleases people! The money changers whom Jesus drove from the temple could undoubtedly have argued that their innovation was popular. But it did not please him because it did not correspond to God's revealed truth (John 2:13–17).

Worship from the heart and according to the book (the Bible)—that is the kind of worship that pleases God. We are not left to define worship for ourselves. The Lord Jesus has defined it for us. — Roger Ellsworth, *Opening up Malachi, Opening Up Commentary* (Leominster: Day One Publications, 2007), 33–34.

17. What do we learn about God from verse 11?

Twice in this verse the Lord says: 'My name shall be great....'

The Lord is absolutely committed to bringing glory to his name! Some find this disturbing. If it is wrong for us to seek our glory, why is it not wrong for God to do the same?

The answer is that it is wrong for us to seek our glory because we are sinners. But God, as a perfect being, must seek his own glory. If God did not seek his glory, he would no longer be perfect!

We are face to face here with an awesome truth. God has made us for his glory, and it is our tremendous privilege to live for his glory. But if we refuse to do so, God will still have his glory! — Roger Ellsworth, *Opening up Malachi, Opening Up Commentary* (Leominster: Day One Publications, 2007), 35.

18. Verse 12, 13. How were they profaning God? What is the lesson for us?

The priests were also sinning against the name of the Lord by openly expressing their unhappiness about having to serve. As they went about their duties they were saying, 'Oh, what a weariness!' To them the service of God was an irksome duty instead of a joyous delight.

The Lord also accuses them of sneering at his service. The word 'sneer' comes from a Hebrew word which means to 'blow away'. We might picture it like this: when someone mentioned their work, they would respond with a heavy sigh, a dismissive wave of the hand and rolling of the eyes. Such a reaction would say it all. The service of the Lord was to them a very burdensome, unhappy thing!

We must not read these words without examining ourselves. Are we doing the same things as these priests? As we go about public worship, do we give the impression that the things of God are exceedingly precious and glorious? Or do we give the impression that we are engaged in an unpleasant obligation that must be taken out of the way as quickly as possible? Do we go about our service to the Lord in such a way that we make it appear to be a very unattractive thing and in such a way that we make the things of the world to be very wonderful? Do we show respect for the preaching of God's Word? Or do we, by laughing and talking with those around us, show contempt for it? — Roger Ellsworth, *Opening up Malachi, Opening Up Commentary* (Leominster: Day One Publications, 2007), 39.

19. Psalm 100.2 says to serve the Lord with gladness. Why is it important that we serve God with gladness?

The inspired command of Psalm 100:2 is, "Serve the LORD with gladness" (NASB). We are not to serve God grudgingly or grimly, but gladly.

In the courts of ancient kings, servants were often executed for nothing more than looking sad in the service of the king. Nehemiah, in 2:2 of the book that bears his name, was grieving over the news he'd heard that Jerusalem was still in ruins despite the return of many Jews from the Babylonian exile. As he was serving food to King Artaxerxes one day, the king said to him, "Why does your face look so sad when you are not ill? This can be nothing but sadness of heart." Because of what that could mean for him, Nehemiah writes, "I was very much afraid." You don't mope or sulk when you serve a king. Not only does it give the appearance that you don't want to serve the king, but it is a statement of dissatisfaction with the way he's running things.

Something is wrong if you can't serve the Lord with gladness. I can understand why the person who serves God only out of obligation doesn't serve with gladness. I can understand why the person who serves God in an attempt to earn his way to Heaven doesn't serve with gladness. But the Christian who gratefully acknowledges what God has done for him for eternity should be able to serve God cheerfully and with joy.

For the believer, serving God is not a burden, it's a privilege. Suppose God let you serve in any political or business position in the world, but wouldn't let you serve in His Kingdom? Suppose He let you choose anyone in the world to serve and know intimately, but wouldn't let you serve Him? Or suppose He let you serve yourself, doing anything you wanted with your life and with no needs or worries, but you could never know God? Even the best of these things is miserable slavery in comparison with the glad privilege of serving God. That's why the psalmist could say, "Better is one day in your courts than a thousand elsewhere; I would rather be a doorkeeper in the house of my God than dwell in the tents of the wicked" (Psalm 84:10).

Do you serve on that church committee with gladness or with gloom? Do you serve your neighbors willingly or reluctantly? Do your kids get the impression from you that serving God is something you really enjoy or merely endure? — Donald S. Whitney, *Spiritual Disciplines for the Christian Life* (Colorado Springs, CO: NavPress, 1991), 119–120.

20. **Summary. What do you want to recall from today's conversation? What is the take-away for you?**

21. **How can we support one another in prayer this week?**

7 Minor Prophets, Lesson #11

Good Questions Have Small Groups Talking

www.joshhunt.com

Malachi 2

OPEN

Let's each share your name and one thing that is on your mind these days.

DIG

1. **Chapter 2 is a warning to priests. What is a priest to do?**

    The call of a priest was to stand before God on behalf of the people and to stand before the people on behalf of God. These priests, however, were so caught up with religion that they weren't providing a true representation of God's Law.

    In Acts 20, Paul told the elders to feed the flock of God. Religious activity is not what ministers are called to do. Bazaars and board meetings are not the calling of true ministry. In the early church, even service was delegated to others in order to free the elders to devote themselves to prayer and the study of the Word (Acts 6). — Jon Courson, *Jon Courson's Application Commentary: Volume Two: Psalms-Malachi* (Nashville, TN: Thomas Nelson, 2006), 925.

2. What privilege did a priest have that others didn't?

We are the bride of Christ. As we behold our Bridegroom, we become like Him. The Bible says, "But we all, with unveiled face, beholding as in a mirror the glory of the Lord, are being transformed into the same image from glory to glory, just as by the Spirit of the Lord." 2 Corinthians 3:18 (NKJV)

Don't miss the opening line, "we all." The phrase is quite explicit in the Greek, and for good reason. In the Old Testament, only priests could come into the presence of God. Actually, it is true today: only priests can come into the presence of God.

Here is the big difference: all believers are priests. We believe in the priesthood of all believers, based on this verse and others: "You also, as living stones, are being built up a spiritual house, a holy priesthood, to offer up spiritual sacrifices acceptable to God through Jesus Christ." 1 Peter 2:5 (NKJV)

"We all" includes you. I might paraphrase it this way (insert your name where I have placed mine), "But Johnny, you can behold the glory of the Lord and be transformed by what you see."

Moses begged for what we take for granted, "Please, show me Your glory." Exodus 33:18 (NKJV) Moses begged for access to God. We all have access:

- Through whom also we have access by faith into this grace in which we stand, and rejoice in hope of the glory of God. Romans 5:2 (NKJV)

- For through Him we both have access by one Spirit to the Father. Ephesians 2:18 (NKJV)

- In whom we have boldness and access with confidence through faith in Him. Ephesians 3:12 (NKJV)

We have access. We all have access. You have access. — Johnny Hunt, *Changed* (Pulpit Press, 2014).

3. How was life more difficult for priests than for others?

Priests received no preferential treatment from the one they claim as Lord for themselves and the one they proclaimed as Lord to their people.

That is clear in this section. In fact, the sin of the priests was especially grievous to the Lord because it led the people astray. "To whom much has been given, much will be expected" is an often stated axiom from the Bible. Much was given to the priests. They were under special covenant with the Lord, the covenant established with Levi. They were chosen and equipped to be leaders (for whom God calls to lead, he equips to lead). Verse 7 states God's expectations: "The lips of a priest ought to preserve knowledge, and from his mouth men should seek instruction." But the priests did not live up to the high honor of their calling, and God was angry. — Eric S. Hartzell, *Haggai, Zechariah, Malachi, The People's Bible* (Milwaukee, WI: Northwestern Pub. House, 1991), 134.

4. Do we have priests today?

This is a point of theology that most evangelicals do not understand. Catholics are much closer to the truth than evangelicals on this one. James 5:16 says, "Therefore confess your sins to each other and pray for each other so that you may be healed." Question: What healing is promised to the person who confesses their sin only to God and never to another human being? Answer: none. No healing is promised to the person who confesses his sin privately to God but never to another human being. Forgiveness, yes (1 John 1:9). Healing, no. Forgiveness has to do with the past. We are forgiven past debts. Healing has to do with the ability to function in the future. Unless we confess our sins to a priest, we will never be healed. The reformation said that Catholics got it wrong because we are all priests. We thought the reformers said we didn't need to confess our sins to anybody. We were wrong, and this subtle mistake cost us our understanding of the good news. We thought we could get healing by confessing our sins only to God and never to another human being. It isn't in the contract. The instructions read otherwise.

Our souls desperately need for someone to hear us out. We need to tell our secrets. We need to get it all out of the closet—not in public—but before a priest. We need a friend to represent God to us. We need a friend that we can tell about our depression, our lust, our greed and our hatred. We need someone who will perform the role of a priest for us. We need someone who will represent God to us. We need someone before whom we can be honest. We need someone to hear us out and say to us, "Your sins are forgiven. You are accepted in God's sight. Everything you have done, thought about, and wanted to do has not diminished God's love for you one little bit."

Until we hear this, we will always wonder. We will always wonder if we are really accepted. We put on our good selves and relate to each other through our masks. That is not bad in itself. We do not have to tell all to everyone. We only need one priest, two at the most.

When we tell our stories and someone represents God to us and is our priest and says, "Your sins are forgiven," we will know the joy of the good news. Still, one thing more is needed. We need to understand the goal. What is the point of Christianity anyway? It is not enough to understand what we were saved from. We need to understand what we were saved for. — Josh Hunt, *You Can Double Your Church In Five Years or Less,* 2000.

5. What complaint did Malachi have against these priests?

Priests who approached their work in a flippant way ("you do not set your heart to honor my name") not only brought trouble to themselves, but they also hurt the people. — Eric S. Hartzell, *Haggai, Zechariah, Malachi, The People's Bible* (Milwaukee, WI: Northwestern Pub. House, 1991), 134.

6. Verse 3 is kind of gross. What is that about?

The offal from sacrificial animals was to be removed from the sanctuary and burnt (Exod. 29:14; Lev. 4:11, etc.), but so revolting to God were those who offered to him sacrifices of no value that they and their offerings were to end up on the dung-heap, excluded from God's presence. It is hardly surprising that the Targum dispensed with the metaphor and translated 'I will make visible on your faces the shame of your crimes'. The imagery was boldly uncomplimentary to those whose birth and training had set them apart for sacred duties, and was no doubt resented. The invective of the eighth-century prophets against the cultus (Isa. 1:11–15; Hos. 4:6–10; Amos 4:4, 5; 5:21–23; Mic. 6:6–8) was polite by comparison. — Joyce G. Baldwin, *Haggai, Zechariah and Malachi: An Introduction and Commentary, vol. 28, Tyndale Old Testament Commentaries* (Downers Grove, IL: InterVarsity Press, 1972), 253.

7. Verses 11, 12. Why was marrying foreign wives a problem? What is the application for us?

The men loving pagan women wasn't a new problem in the Jewish nation. When the Jews left Egypt, there was a "mixed multitude" that left with them (Ex. 12:38), which suggests that some Jews had married Egyptian spouses (Lev. 24:10; Num. 11:4). The Jews sinned greatly when they mixed with the women of Midian at Baal Peor (Num. 25), and God judged them severely. Ezra (Ezra 9:1–4) and Nehemiah (Neh. 13:23–31) had to contend with this problem, and it's not totally absent from the church today (2 Cor. 6:14–18).

In divorcing their Jewish wives and marrying pagan women, the men were committing several sins. To begin with, it was treachery as they broke their vows to God and to their wives. They were profaning God's covenant and treating it as nothing. Not only had the Lord given specific requirements for marriage in His Law (Ex. 34:11–16; Deut. 7:3–4), but the covenant of marriage was built into creation. "Have we not all one father?" (Mal. 2:10) refers to God as the Father of all humans, the Creator (Acts. 17:28). God made man and women for each other and established marriage for the good of the human family. So, what these men did was contrary to what God had written into nature and in His covenant. — Warren W. Wiersbe, *Be Amazed, "Be" Commentary Series* (Wheaton, IL: Victor Books, 1996), 148–149.

8. 2 Corinthians 6.14 – 18 is a good cross-reference. What does it mean to be unequally yoked? Why is it a problem?

Again, this doesn't mean that believers should avoid contact with people of other religions or philosophies. In fact, Paul wholeheartedly encouraged close association with others as a means of demonstrating the love of God. If, however, these individuals maintain an evil lifestyle, it's only a matter of time before their troubles become our troubles. To illustrate his point, Paul quotes a pagan playwright in 1 Corinthians 15:33: "Bad company corrupts good character" (Menander, Thais 218).

Immorality is poisonous. You can never become immune to its deadly potency. It's like sewage spewing from a cesspool; it contaminates everything close by. — Charles R. Swindoll, *Abraham: One Nomad's Amazing Journey of Faith* (Carol Stream, IL: Tyndale, 2014).

9. Verse 13. What was wrong with flooding God's altar with tears?

After committing these sins, the men then brought offerings to the Lord and wept at the altar (vv. 12–13), seeking His help and blessing. Perhaps they had the idea that they could sin blatantly with the intention of coming to God for forgiveness. But if they were truly repentant, they would have forsaken their heathen wives and taken their true wives back, which is what Ezra made them do (Ezra 9–10). These men were guilty of hypocritical worship that had nothing to do with a changed heart. Instead of forgiving them, God was ready to "cut them off." — Warren W. Wiersbe, *Be Amazed, "Be" Commentary Series* (Wheaton, IL: Victor Books, 1996), 149.

10. How does your translation have verse 16?

But there is one further compelling factor: For I hate divorce, says the Lord. English Versions agree that this is the prophet's meaning, even though the Hebrew in fact reads 'if he hates send (her) away', a sense found also in the ancient Versions. Evidently the text suffered early at the hands of some who wanted to bring Malachi's teaching into line with that of Deuteronomy 24:1, which permitted divorce. Such a reading undermines all that the prophet is seeking to convey. The God of Israel, a name used only here by Malachi, is appropriate because the subject concerns the future of the chosen race. He sees divorce to be like covering one's garment with violence, a figurative expression for all kinds of gross injustice which, like the blood of a murdered victim, leave their mark for all to see.

JB makes the last sentence very meaningful: Respect your own life, therefore, and do not break faith like this. It is in the best interests of the individual as well as of the community that families should not be broken by divorce. Malachi's plea prepares the way for the teaching of Jesus (Matt. 5:31, 32; 19:4–9). — Joyce G. Baldwin, *Haggai, Zechariah and Malachi: An Introduction and Commentary, vol. 28, Tyndale Old Testament Commentaries* (Downers Grove, IL: InterVarsity Press, 1972), 262.

11. Verse 16. How does God think differently about divorce than do people today?

Regardless of cultural acceptance, divorce is not normal, nor is it neutral, nor is it a pious promise of an easy way out of conflict. Divorce has always been destructive. Its consequences have always been far-reaching and long-lasting. Though sometimes, admittedly, it is permitted. — Charles R. Swindoll, *Getting through the Tough Stuff: It's Always Something!* (Nashville: Thomas Nelson, 2004).

12. Why does God hate divorce?

The Bible says that God hates divorce (Malachi 2.16). Ever wonder why?

Because God has been through divorce, and he knows firsthand how awful it is. We serve a divorced God. Jeremiah 3: 8 states: "I gave faithless Israel her certificate of divorce and sent her away because of all her adulteries." God knows all about divorce and its shame, failure, rejection, loneliness, and sadness.

How do you picture God? Do you picture him as a judge banging his gavel on the desk in front of him? Do you picture him as a scientist and you as his laboratory experiment? Do you picture him as a busy executive or a free-wheeling millionaire who does not have much time to think of you? Do you picture him as an absent-minded professor who can't remember your name?

God is pictured in the Bible as a jilted lover who longs to be in relationship with His bride. He longs to be reconciled to you and to the people who you serve through your micro-church, the small group.

Reconciliation has always been somewhat of a sterile, religious term to me. I knew that we reconciled a bank book but was never quite sure how that related to being reconciled with God. Since my divorce, reconciliation has taken on a whole new meaning to me.

I remember consciously thinking that I would give anything to be reconciled to my wife. I love my job, but I would gladly give it up to get her back. I love traveling, speaking, writing, and producing videos, but I would gladly give it all up to be reconciled. I enjoy my trinkets, toys, gadgets, and gizmos, but I would gladly give them all up to be reconciled with her.

I got to thinking, what is the most valuable thing in my life? Would I give it up? I thought about my kids. Would I give up the life of one of my kids to be reconciled to her? I thought I would. I thought, I would give up the life of one of my kids to be reconciled.

(Please note, this was a passing feeling, not an ongoing one nor a stable intention. I am just describing a passing feeling.)

I think the day I thought those thoughts for the first time, I came very close to understanding the heart of God. He didn't just think about giving up the life of His Son to be reconciled, He actually did it. It was not just a passing thing, but an ongoing feeling and a stable intention, and he actually did it. He counted a relationship with you and me so valuable that he was willing to let His Son die so that we could be reconciled. — Josh Hunt, *10 Marks of Incredible Small Group Leaders,* 2005.

13. Why do you think divorce is so common today?

I'm often asked what I perceive to be the greatest threat to families today. I could talk, in response, about alcoholism, drug abuse, infidelity, and the other common causes of divorce. But there is another curse that accounts for more family breakups than the others combined. It is the simple matter of overcommitment and the tyranny of the urgent.

Husbands and wives who fill their lives with never-ending volumes of work are too exhausted to take walks together, to share their deeper feelings, to understand and meet each other's needs. They're even too worn out to have a meaningful sexual relationship, because fatigue is a destroyer of desire.

This breathless pace predominates in millions of households, leaving every member of the family frazzled and irritable. Husbands are moonlighting to bring home more money. Wives are on their own busy career track. Children are often ignored, and life goes speeding by in a deadly routine. Even some grandparents are too busy to keep the grandkids. I see this kind of overcommitment as the quickest route to the destruction of the family. And there simply must be a better way.

Some friends of mine recently sold their house and moved into a smaller and less expensive place just so they could lower their payments and reduce the hours required in the workplace. That kind of downward mobility is almost unheard of today—it's almost un-American. But when we reach the end of our lives and we look back on the things that mattered most, those precious relationships with people we love will rank at the top of the list.

If friends and family will be a treasure to us then, why not live like we believe it today? That may be the best advice I have ever given anyone—and the most difficult to implement. — J. F. Dobson, *Dr. Dobson's Handbook of Family Advice: Encouragement and Practical Help for Your Home* (Eugene, OR: Harvest House, 2012).

14. What pain comes to those who divorce?

In the 1960s, the surgeon general declared cigarettes harmful to the smoker's health. More recently, researchers have warned us about the dangers of foods high in fat and cholesterol. But we hear less about the health hazards of divorce.

Many studies have revealed the emotional and financial impact of divorce on couples and their children. But less well known is the research showing that divorce puts people at a high risk for psychiatric problems and physical disease.

Dr. David Larson, psychiatrist and researcher in Washington DC, reviewed medical studies on this subject and made some startling discoveries. For instance, being divorced and a nonsmoker is only slightly less dangerous than smoking a pack or more a day and staying married. Also, every type of terminal cancer strikes divorced individuals of both sexes more frequently than it does married people. What's more, premature death rates are significantly higher among divorced men and women. Physicians believe this is because the emotional trauma of divorce stresses the body and lowers the immune system's defense against disease.

In the light of this evidence, perhaps the surgeon general should consider warning married couples about the potential health risks of divorce. Certainly, healthy families are more beneficial to the well-being of children. — J. F. Dobson, *Dr. Dobson's Handbook of Family Advice: Encouragement and Practical Help for Your Home* (Eugene, OR: Harvest House, 2012).

15. What price do children pay when parents divorce?

Divorce carries lifelong negative implications for children.

It's now known that emotional development in children is directly related to the presence of warm, nurturing, sustained, and continuous interaction with both parents. Anything that interferes with the vital relationship with either mother or father can have lasting consequences for the child.

One landmark study revealed that 90 percent of children from divorced homes suffered from an acute sense of shock when the separation occurred, including profound grieving and irrational fears. Fifty percent reported feeling rejected and abandoned, and indeed half of the fathers never came to see their children three years after the divorce. One-third of the boys and girls feared abandonment by the remaining parent, and 66 percent experienced yearning for the absent parent with an intensity that researchers described as overwhelming. Most significantly, 37 percent of the children were even more unhappy and dissatisfied five years after the divorce than they had been at eighteen months. In other words, time did not heal their wounds.

That's the real meaning of divorce. It is certainly what I think about, with righteous indignation, when I see infidelity and marital deceit portrayed on television as some kind of exciting game for two. Some excitement. Some game.
— J. F. Dobson, Dr. Dobson's Handbook of Family Advice: Encouragement and Practical Help for Your Home (Eugene, OR: Harvest House, 2012).

16. Does lack of conflict mean we have little chance for divorce?

The first step to managing conflict is not doing what is destructive. Our national survey of over 50,000 couples found that the number one stumbling block to resolving conflict is conflict avoidance: At least one partner in nearly two-thirds (63 percent) of the couples in our study admitted to going out of their way to avoid conflict with their partner. As discussed in chapter 10, this only allows for a buildup of debris in the relationship. Every couple has periods of time when a small buildup occurs in their relationship, but when at least one partner habitually tiptoes around issues with the other, the couple is sure to find their pile of debris growing larger over time. It can then be easily set ablaze by the simplest of issues.

Why do persons avoid conflict? To avoid hurting their partner's feelings (something at least one partner does in 52 percent of all couples) and to end an argument (56 percent of couples). The irony is that while a quick end to an argument reduces tension immediately, many studies demonstrate that it only extends and expands the conflict later on.[3] Again, a small fire properly dealt with now is much better than dousing the fire too soon only to have it rage out of control later.

The second most common stumbling block for couples is one or both partners usually feeling solely responsible for the problems they argue about. The truth is both partners usually have some responsibility for conflict; each contributes something at some point. But resentment is sure to grow if one partner is made to feel the blame most of the time. Marital conflicts become a repeating story of "I win, you lose." Instead of feeling safe to explore the issue at hand, this dynamic sets up a competition where everyone loses in the end. — Ron L. Deal and David H. Olson, *The Remarriage Checkup* (Grand Rapids, MI: Baker, 2010).

17. What are some practical things we can do to prevent divorce?

Discussing five movies about relationships over a month could cut the three-year divorce rate for newlyweds in half, researchers report. The study, involving 174 couples, is the first long-term investigation to compare different types of early marriage intervention programs.

The findings show that an inexpensive, fun, and relatively simple movie-and-talk approach can be just as effective as other more intensive therapist-led methods—reducing the divorce or separation rate from 24 to 11 percent after three years.

"We thought the movie treatment would help, but not nearly as much as the other programs in which we were teaching all of these state-of-the-art skills," said Ronald Rogge, associate professor of psychology at the University of Rochester and lead author of the study. "The results suggest that husbands and wives have a pretty good sense of what they might be doing right and wrong in their relationships. Thus, you might not need to teach them a whole lot of skills to cut the divorce rate. You might just need to get them to think about how they are currently behaving. And for five movies to give us a benefit over three years—that is awesome." http://www.rochester.edu/news/divorce-rate-cut-in-half-for-couples-who-discussed-relationship-movies/

18. What advice would you have for a young couple who wanted a long, happy marriage?

From time to time, I post about what makes for a happy, long-term marriage or partnership. In the past, I've written about the importance of sharing similar interests, having complementary skill sets and even how much you smiled in photographs when you were younger.

But lately, I've stumbled across some interesting new research on the topic which I thought I'd share.

Here are five ways to avoid divorce:

1. Be thrifty. A recent study of 1,734 married couples revealed that couples who don't value money very highly score 10 to 15 percent better on marriage stability and other measures of relationship quality than couples where one or both are materialistic. According to Jason Carroll, a professor at BYU and the lead author of the study, materialistic couples exhibit "eroding communication, poor conflict resolution and low responsiveness to each other."

2. Work (especially wives). Ironically enough, feminism has also been very good for marital health and stability. At least according to Stephanie Coontz, a scholar of history and family studies who has written extensively on marriage in the United States. In her book, A Strange Stirring: The Feminine

Mystique and American Women at the Dawn of the 1960s, Coontz argues that the changes that Betty Friedan and other feminists of her time agitated for have actually been good for marriage. The divorce rate has fallen and actually tends "to be lowest in states where more than 70 percent of married women work outside the home," Coontz reports. What's more, "The specialization into separate gender roles that supposedly stabilized marriages in the 1950s and 1960s, actually raises the risk of divorce today." Working outside the home, says Coontz, is also good for a couple's sex life.

A recent study from the Pew Research Center also aserts that working wives are beneficial to marriages. This study showed that shifts within marriages -- specifically, men taking on more housework and women earning more outside the home -- have contributed to lower divorce rates and happier unions. One couple found that just shifting their traditional gender roles each summer did a lot to strengthen their marriage.

3. Spend time apart. More counter-intuitive wisdom. I think that some couples make the mistake of thinking that the true sign of a happy couple is wanting to do every last thing together. Wrong. Yes, it's important to have a lot of overlapping interests. But, as I've noted before, you also need to keep a private space -- a room of one's own, as it were. This is the main message of Iris Krasnow's new book, "The Secret Lives of Wives", which is based on interviews with more than 200 women from different educational, social, and economic brackets, all of whom are in long-term marriages (15-plus years). In addition to sex (see below), many pointed to the importance of prolonged separations from their spouses as crucial to making these partnerships last. The reasoning? Physical distance makes women more emotionally and physically self-reliant and also (surprisingly, perhaps) enhances communication between partners.

4. Have sex. Just make that sure you don't spend too much time apart. According to a recent article on The Huffington Post, there are more than 17,000 people who identify with "I Live In a Sexless Marriage" on the Experience Project. But if recent surveys are correct, the author speculates that this

number doesn't even come close to the actual figure, which she estimates as closer to 20 million married Americans. Moreover, couples who are dissatisfied with their sex life are more likely to consider divorce and/or term their marriage "unhappy." D.A. Wolf certainly hit a nerve when she posted on the importance of sex within a long-term relationship on the Huffington Post's Divorce vertical last weekend. Have a gander at the comments section. Wowza.

5. Do small, recognizable actions. I was absolutely fascinated by this interview in Slate with New York Times health blogger Tara Parker-Pope about her book For Better: The Science of a Good Marriage. In it, Parker-Pope reveals that a lot of research shows that the main determinants of happy, sustained marriages are actually small, tangible things like having have at least five small positive interactions (touching, smiling, paying a compliment) for every negative one (sneering, eye rolling, withdrawal), the presence/absence of sleep problems, how you treat your partner during the first three minutes of a fight, and my own personal favorite: how you recount your own "How We Met" narrative. Phew. At least I have that one covered.

http://www.huffingtonpost.com/delia-lloyd/5-ways-to-avoid-divorce_b_1019194.html

19. What do you want to recall from today's conversation?

20. How can we support one another in prayer this week?

7 Minor Prophets, Lesson #12

Good Questions Have Small Groups Talking

www.joshhunt.com

Malachi 3

OPEN

Let's each share your name and one thing that is on your mind these days.

DIG

1. **Malachi 3.1. Who is meant by the messenger in this passage?**

   "My messenger"—John the Baptist (Mal. 3:1a). As we've seen, the name Malachi means "my messenger"; and the messenger referred to in this statement we know as John the Baptist. Speaking of John the Baptist, Jesus said, "For this is he of whom it is written, 'Behold, I send My messenger before Your face who will prepare Your way before You' " (Matt. 11:10, NKJV; see Mark 1:2 and Luke 7:27).

   While Malachi was the last of the writing prophets, John the Baptist was the last and the greatest of the Old Covenant prophets. To John was given the unique privilege of ministering at the close of the old dispensation and the beginning of the new, and it was John who presented Jesus to Israel (John 1:29–31). Like Jeremiah and Ezekiel, John was born into a priestly family but was called of God to be a prophet. He was also a martyr, for he gave his life in the work God called him to do (Matt. 14:1–12).

The Prophet Isaiah had also written about John's ministry (Isa. 40:3–5; Mark 1:3; Luke 3:4–6; John 1:23). The image is that of people preparing a way for the king to come, leveling the roads and removing the obstacles so that the king might enjoy an easy and comfortable trip. John prepared the way for the ministry of Jesus by preaching the Word to the crowds, urging them to repent of their sins, baptizing them, and then introducing them to Jesus. — Warren W. Wiersbe, *Be Amazed, "Be" Commentary Series* (Wheaton, IL: Victor Books, 1996), 153–154.

2. What does "the day of His coming" refer to?

3:2. Verse 1 describes events at the time of Christ's first coming, whereas verses 2-6 depict Christ's judgment on the world at his second advent. According to Alden, "Like most of the Old Testament prophets, Malachi, in his picture of the coming Christ, mingled the two advents" (Alden, Expositor's Bible Commentary, 719; cp. Zech. 9:9-10). Malachi's countrymen complained that injustice was rampant and the wicked seemed to go free. Messiah would remedy this situation. As a refiner's fire purges dross from the silver (v. 3) and a launderer's soap cleanses impurities from clothing, all wickedness would be eradicated from the earth at Christ's return. Who can endure the day of his coming? Who can stand when he appears? The answer is, only those who have repented and believed in the Messiah. "The day of his coming" is the day of the Lord. — *Holman Old Testament Commentary – Nahum-Malachi.*

3. Verse 7. How do we return to God?

How would the people return? In this case, it would be through giving. Why? Giving is not God's way of raising money. It's His way of raising kids. You see, because we're sinners, each of us has the tendency to be selfish, small, greedy, and material. But God is a giver (John 3:16) and He wants His children to be like Him.

In the Bible, there are over four hundred fifty verses on faith and over five hundred fifty verses on prayer. But there are over 2,100 verses on giving. One of every ten verses in the New Testament deals with giving, money, or possessions. Of the thirty-eight parables Jesus taught, sixteen deal directly with giving, money, or possession. Why is the Lord so emphatic about this? Because Jesus said that wherever a man's treasure is, there will his heart be also (Luke 12:34). He wants us to give to Him—not because He needs our money but because He wants our heart. — Jon Courson, *Jon Courson's Application Commentary: Volume Two: Psalms-Malachi* (Nashville, TN: Thomas Nelson, 2006), 927.

4. **Malachi 3.8ff. What does this passage teach about tithing?**

In this passage, God clues us in to three important truths about the tithe. First of all, if we are not tithing, we are robbing him. Partial obedience is complete disobedience. That's why it is not a good idea to stay at basic-level giving. While it's a great place to get started, it's not yet in the realm of obedience.

Can you imagine if a husband approached his wife and asked, "Honey, have you been faithful to me?" and she replied, "Well, partially. I've only committed adultery half of the last fifty-two weeks." That wouldn't work, would it? Partial obedience is complete disobedience.

Let me take this opportunity to define the tithe, just to clear up any uncertainty. A tithe literally means the first tenth. We are commanded to return one-tenth of our income to God—but not just any tenth. We are to give back the first tenth of all God blesses us with each time we are paid. In Proverbs 3:9–10, Scripture teaches us, "Honor the LORD with your possessions, and with the firstfruits of all your increase; so your barns will be filled with plenty, and your vats will overflow with new wine" (NKJV, emphasis added). Giving leftovers won't do. God wants the best of what we have to offer. — Nelson Searcy and Jennifer Dykes Henson, *The Generosity Ladder: Your Next Step to Financial Peace* (Grand Rapids, MI: Baker Books, 2010), 57.

5. **Would you guess that Christian people are more or less generous than non-Christians?**

Conservative Christians put their money where their mouth is when it comes to giving. That's according to a study from Syracuse University published in 2006 by Arthur Brooks in Who Really Cares: The Surprising Truth about Compassionate Conservatism. "If you asked me, I would have expected to find that religious conservatives are stingy," said Brooks, a committed Catholic and political independent. "That's what we are told all the time." What he found instead was that conservative Christians give more in "every measurable way," from writing checks to volunteering time to donating blood.

Brooks attributes the difference to four factors: church attendance, two-parent families, a Protestant work ethic, and distaste for government social services. Of those, church attendance is the most telling. Ninety-one percent of regular church attendees give to charity each year, compared with 66 percent of those who said they do not have a religion. The gap adds up—the faithful give four times more money per year than their secular counterparts. While most of that money is given to churches, religious people also give more to a secular charity such as the Red Cross or to their alma mater.

Religious people also donate twice as much blood and are more likely to "behave in compassionate ways toward strangers," Brooks said. For example, they are much more likely to return extra change to a cashier when they are accidentally given too much.

Generous giving is part of the religious conservative identity, according to sociologist Tony Campolo. "The Religious Right, by conviction, is convinced that helping the poor is something that should be done individually or by the church," said Campolo. "[They say that] asking the state to do it is wrong." — Craig Brian Larson and Phyllis Ten Elshof, *1001 Illustrations That Connect* (Grand Rapids, MI: Zondervan Publishing House, 2008), 95–96.

6. How much do the average Christian give?

The average modern-day Christian gives only 2.5 percent of his income, which obviously is nowhere close to a tithe. In Money, Possessions, and Eternity, Alcorn writes, "When we as New Testament believers, living in a far more affluent society than ancient Israel, give only a fraction of that given by the poorest Old Testament believers, we surely must reevaluate our concept of 'grace giving.' And when you consider that we have the indwelling of the Spirit of God and they didn't, the contrast becomes even more glaring." We seem to have a heart problem.

Could the problem be that, deep down, many of those who oppose the tithe do so not out of biblical knowledge, prayer, and deduction but out of misinformation or out of their own sinful (perhaps even subconscious) desire to be the master of their money?

Their hearts are tied to their wallets, as are all of ours, and the contents of those wallets aren't being poured into God's work. So it makes sense that their hearts—far from understanding the supernatural blessings associated with the practical funding of God's kingdom—are waging a war for financial control.

As a result, they fight against the tithe. They call tithing outdated and legalistic. Even if only subconsciously, they feel that if they can discount the biblical mandate for twenty-first-century Jesus followers to tithe, then they can continue to handle their money as they please. The majority of these people are not intentionally choosing to be selfish. They are just caught up in a problem of the heart—one that is often caused more by a lack of knowledge about the tithe than by willful disobedience. — Nelson Searcy and Jennifer Dykes Henson, *The Generosity Ladder: Your Next Step to Financial Peace* (Grand Rapids, MI: Baker Books, 2010), 70–71.

7. What blessings come to the generous?

The second thing we can learn from Malachi 3:8–10 is that those who are not tithing are not being fully blessed by God.

Scripture actually tells us that non-tithers are "under a curse" (3:9). In other words, failing to tithe blocks God's ability to bless us to the extent he would like.

What does this curse look like in our culture? Here are a few of the trademark symptoms:

- Going to bed every night worried about money
- Arguing with your spouse over money
- Living in fear of losing everything

No man can mock God. We cannot ignore and dispute his plan for our livelihood and still expect to have his blessing on our life. But when we are obedient to the call to tithe, he will bless us in unimaginable ways—both financially and otherwise. I have learned firsthand that I would rather tithe 10 percent and live with God's supernatural blessing on the other 90 percent than to have the full 100 percent in my pocket and operate without God's blessing.

On a side note, one of the most frequently asked questions I hear about tithing is, "Should I tithe based on my gross income or my net income?" My answer is always the same: "Which amount do you want God to bless?" When you make a decision to tithe based on your net income, you are essentially putting the government in a position of priority over God. You are giving to him from what's left over after Uncle Sam takes his due. Giving based on what the government leaves behind is not a tithe. — Nelson Searcy and Jennifer Dykes Henson, *The Generosity Ladder: Your Next Step to Financial Peace* (Grand Rapids, MI: Baker Books, 2010), 58–59.

8. Verse 10. What exactly does he mean, "Test me"?

Third, Malachi 3 is the only place in all of Scripture where God says "test me" in a positive way. He is essentially saying, "Bring me the tithe and see if I don't bless you. Go ahead. Try it." His challenge here is to Christians and non-Christians alike.

At the church I pastor in New York City, The Journey Church, we sometimes issue a tithe challenge to people, and we direct it at both believers and nonbelievers. I teach what God says about the tithe, as we've been discussing here, and then ask people to test God in his promise by committing to tithe for a short period of time, usually four months.

In issuing the challenge, I will go so far as to say, "Hey, if you think you don't believe in God, isn't it worth a few dollars of your income over the next few months to prove once and for all that he doesn't exist? You are staking your eternity on this, so why not? Why don't you tithe for a few months, and if you still think God doesn't exist, you can live the rest of your life without having to worry about it." God said to test him. — Nelson Searcy and Jennifer Dykes Henson, *The Generosity Ladder: Your Next Step to Financial Peace* (Grand Rapids, MI: Baker Books, 2010), 60–61.

9. Have you ever tested God? How did it work out?

One time I met a gentleman at The Journey who was a self-professed agnostic. Let's call him Ben. Ben happened to be visiting with a friend one fall Sunday when I laid out this tithe challenge. Ben was a little older than our average attenders, and he was in the midst of a successful career as an air traffic controller.

After the service, Ben came over to me and said, "Okay. I'm going to test God. I want to take this 'tithe challenge' and dispel all this foolishness. I'm going to prove to you that God doesn't exist."

So he and I sat down and figured out what 10 percent of his income would be and divided that out over the next four months. He came to church a couple of times during the course of the challenge but not regularly. His tithing, however, was like clockwork. Can you guess what happened?

God worked in Ben's life in amazing ways. He began being blessed, both tangibly and intangibly. To make a long story short, Ben came back to me after those four months fully convinced of God's existence. Of course, as usually happens when someone takes the tithe challenge, he has continued to tithe.

Ben is not an exception to the rule. I have seen this scenario play out time and time again. God shows up in people's lives when they honor him. He has obligated himself to do so. God's promise about tithing is an if/then promise. "If you honor me with your firstfruits, then I will pour out my blessing in your life."

God's promise of blessing crosses over into the New Testament. Recall Jesus's "of course you should tithe" comment in Matthew 23:23. Paul follows that up in 2 Corinthians 8:7: "Since you excel in so many ways—in your faith, your gifted speakers, your knowledge, your enthusiasm, and your love for us—I want you to excel also in this gracious act of giving." As we excel in grace, we should excel in giving. — Nelson Searcy and Jennifer Dykes Henson, *The Generosity Ladder: Your Next Step to Financial Peace* (Grand Rapids, MI: Baker Books, 2010), 61–62.

10. What is meant by "the storehouse"?

Often people question not the amount of a proper gift but where it should be given. Some people believe they should be able to distribute their tithe as they see fit. They want to control how their money is spent. If they aren't happy with the way their local church handles its finances, they think they should have the freedom to give their tithe to an outside organization. But Scripture teaches us that the tithe is to go to the local church—the one and only organization that is eternal. Offerings, any giving over and above the tithe, can be given outside the church, but not the tithe.

Let's look again at Malachi 3. God says to bring the whole tithe into the storehouse. Why? So "there may be food in my house" (v. 10 NIV). In biblical times, the storehouse referred to the temple. Today it is the modern church. The "food" God refers to is the ministry of the temple or, as we understand it, the ongoing work of God through his church on this earth.

In the New Testament church, givers actually laid their gifts at the apostles' feet, trusting them to distribute the money as God directed. Consider Paul's words in Acts 4:34–35: "Those who owned land or houses sold them, brought the money from the sales and put it at the apostles' feet, and it was distributed to anyone as he had need" (NIV). Can you imagine having to place your tithe at the feet of your local church leader? That would be intimidating, to say the least. Thank goodness we have more modern options for giving to the church—we can give at a service, online, or by mailing an envelope to the church office, to name a few—but the principle still holds true: we bring the tithe to our local, spiritually qualified leaders, and they distribute the money for God's work.

The tithe is specifically intended to infuse the local church so that God's kingdom can continue to expand at the best possible rate. It is not up to you and me as givers to judge where we'd like to give our tithe. We are simply told to make it the firstfruits, make it proportional, and bring it to the storehouse. In Money, Possessions, and Eternity, Randy Alcorn writes:

> I'm often asked, "But how can I give to my church [if] I don't agree with how the money is spent?" Perhaps your church leaders are in a better position to judge this than you are.... If the Bible tells me to pay taxes (Rom. 13:1–7), and I comply even though some will be wasted and even used for bad purposes, surely I can give to God even when I don't feel comfortable with every use of the funds.

Of course, you do have to be wise. If you feel your church is operating in opposition to the Bible or truly misusing funds, you should talk to the leaders about your concerns. If you still don't feel comfortable tithing to your church, you may need to begin seeking God's direction on finding a new church where you can give as he commands. A church leader's misuse of funds doesn't negate your call to tithe to the local church. Make sure you are in an environment where you can obey God fully. — Nelson Searcy and Jennifer Dykes Henson,

The Generosity Ladder: Your Next Step to Financial Peace (Grand Rapids, MI: Baker Books, 2010), 62–65.

11. What exactly does "tithe" mean?

The Old Testament called the tithe the "first fruits." It was called the first fruits because the people were to give first. They didn't have money as we do today, so they would give part of their harvest— the first part of their harvest. They would give the first lamb born of the flock.

They did not do what people sometimes do today— pay anybody and everybody first, before they do their giving. I will make a promise to you: you will never be a generous giver if you give to God last. You will never be a generous giver if you give to God your leftovers.

Malachi 3:10 speaks of the tithes and the offerings. "Tithe" simply means "tenth." Offerings are what we give above the tithe.

The tithe is the starting point. Offerings are given above the tithe. If you tithe, I applaud your generosity. Still, I would invite you to see that in the Bible, the tithe is the starting point, not the finish line of giving. It is the floor, not the ceiling.

Here's what we do, and what we recommend for you to do: when you get paid, make the first check beginning check. (Better to make an automatic draft as discussed above.)

Many people do the opposite. They get paid, and they start paying their bills. They pay their electric bill, their mortgage, their cell phone bill, the jetski payment, and so on. If they have anything left, they give to God. This is not the biblical pattern. — Brad Whitt, Rooted

12. Some people say that tithing is an Old Testament concept. What do you think?

Some of you may be interested in diving a little deeper into the tithing debate. In broad terms, the divide over tithing comes down to a debate concerning legalism versus grace.

Opponents say that tithing, which has been in existence since the beginning of man (Gen. 14:20; Lev. 27:30–33) and was a command of the Jewish law (Num. 18:28–29; Deut. 12:11), was abolished when Jesus came on the scene. But Scripture confirms that Jesus came to earth to fulfill the law, not to dismiss it. Jesus himself minces no words when he says:

> Don't misunderstand why I have come. I did not come to abolish the law of Moses or the writings of the prophets. No, I came to accomplish their purpose. I tell you the truth, until heaven and earth disappear, not even the smallest detail of God's law will disappear until its purpose is achieved. So if you ignore the least commandment and teach others to do the same, you will be called the least in the Kingdom of Heaven. But anyone who obeys God's laws and teaches them will be called great in the Kingdom of Heaven. (Matt. 5:17–19)

Jesus shifted the heart of humankind from legalism to grace, but in doing so he in no way rendered the law obsolete.

I'm sure you are familiar with Jesus's most famous teaching, the Sermon on the Mount. Even if you've never read the account for yourself, I guarantee you know a lot about what he says. The words have become part of our culture. In this teaching, Jesus magnifies rather than minimizes the expectations previously associated with the law of Moses.

He says, and I paraphrase, "You've heard that you shouldn't murder. Well, I say don't even be angry with anyone. You know that you shouldn't commit adultery, but guess what? Under grace, you have already done so if you even look at a woman lustfully." The expectations Jesus places on his followers, thanks to the introduction of grace, go above and beyond the expectations of the law that preceded him.

If anger is now even with murder and lust is even with adultery, doesn't it stand to reason that the tithe should now be considered a base-level command—a minimum expectation now maximized through grace, like the other components of the law? Rather than being obsolete, giving under grace implies that we should give even more sacrificially than those who gave under the law; we should operate at a level higher than the threshold previously mandated.

Even under the bondage of the law, devout Jews often took it upon themselves to give God more than the first 10 percent of their increase. They recognized the truth that we've discovered in our paradigm shift: all they had came from God.

Logic would then suggest that we who have been given so much would also recognize the source of our blessings and feel even more inclined to return the tithe as an act of worship. After all, that's what tithing truly is; it's an act of worship. We should easily recognize 10 percent as simple obedience—like we recognize not murdering and not committing adultery as simple obedience—and be filled with the desire to give at least that much. Unfortunately, this is not the case. — Nelson Searcy and Jennifer Dykes Henson, *The Generosity Ladder: Your Next Step to Financial Peace* (Grand Rapids, MI: Baker Books, 2010), 67–70.

13. Is this saying that God will bless us financially as we give or is this talking about a spiritual blessing?

Do you ever feel like your paycheck is just being eaten up? Through Haggai, the Lord said, "You put your money into bags with holes. Your budget isn't working because, although you're building your own houses, you've neglected My work" (1:6). Tithing makes good sense because God isn't going to be your debtor. You'll never be able to give more to Him than He'll give back to you. He'll never "owe you one." — Jon Courson, *Jon Courson's Application Commentary: Volume Two: Psalms-Malachi* (Nashville, TN: Thomas Nelson, 2006), 928.

14. When have you seen God open the windows of Heaven? Who has a story?

My (JCD's) dad, an evangelist, was the original soft touch. I remember him once going off to speak in a tiny church and coming home ten days later. Eventually my mother asked about the offering. I can still see my father's face as he smiled and looked at the floor.

"You gave the money away again, didn't you?" she asked.

"Myrt," he said, "the pastor there is going through a hard time. His kids are so needy. I felt I should give the entire fifty dollars to them."

My good mother looked at my father for a few moments and then smiled. "You know, if God told you to do it, it's okay with me."

A few days later, we ran completely out of money, so my father gathered us for a time of prayer. He said, "Lord, you told us that if we would honor you in our good times, that you would take care of us when things are difficult. We need a little help at this time." The next day we received an unexpected check for $1,200. That's the way it happened—not once, but many times. No matter what you give, you'll find you can never outgive God. — James C. Dobson and Shirley Dobson, *Night Light: A Devotional for Couples* (Carol Stream, IL: Tyndale, 2011).

15. In addition to giving to the church, how else should we give?

This is the statement of a lavish God, who is ready to pour out his blessing upon us . . . but we also must have God's lavish heart.

Ever hear someone say, "If there is a God, why does he allow people to starve in Africa?" I want to shoot back the question, "Why do you allow it?" You see, God uses ordinary people to do extraordinary things in others' lives. And you can be a part of that—in a small or large way.

But it takes stepping outside yourself, taking a risk, and looking for others' needs. So many of us complain about what we don't have instead of acknowledging what we do have and thanking God for those blessings.

Each day is a gift, but how we spend that gift is up to us. Gifts and talents should never be used only for ourselves.

I believe wholeheartedly in something I call natural tithing. If you see a need in someone's life and you can meet it right then, do it. If you can do it anonymously, all the better. For example, if a person needs a meal, and you have seven bucks in your pocket and can buy him a Big Mac at McDonald's, complete with fries and a Coke, do so. (Or, for a lower cholesterol version, try Subway.) Give a little, and you'll be amazed at how your own perspective on life will improve. The famous coach John Wooden said, "You can't live a perfect day without doing something for someone who will never be able to repay you."[24]

Although I always strive to do the right thing, I find myself, like Saint Paul, sometimes doing what I don't want to do: Bypassing the needy when I'm in a rush. Brushing off those who rub me the wrong way. Or thinking, What if that person uses the money to buy a cheap bottle of muscatel instead of food? What others do with what you give them is up to them. What's up to you is learning to have the heart of a natural tither—a lavish giver.

Let's face it: we're all flawed to the core. There are some people you'll like and feel comfortable with; there are others you'll have a hard time liking, much less loving.

But Jesus said, "Whatever you did for one of the least of these brothers of mine, you did for me."[25] If we remember that every person is a creation of Almighty God and turn our hearts toward natural tithing, God will bring us prosperity of heart, mind, and finances so we can lavish even more on others.

When we do the right thing, not the expedient or cheap thing, we become more like Jesus, who gave lavishly.

Now that's indeed something you can take to the bank . . . eternally. — Kevin Leman, *Way of the Wise, the: Simple Truths for Living Well* (Grand Rapids, MI: Baker, 2013).

16. Would you guess the generous are measurably happier?

Boston, MA (AHN) - A recent survey revealed that those who spend a reasonable amount of money on other people experience greater elation than those who buy things for themselves. Scientists from the Harvard Business School gathered 632 Americans and questioned them about their income, their spending habits, and their level of happiness.

Separately, the experts gathered 16 professionals up for a bonus between $3,000 and $8,000, and asked them similar questions six to eight weeks before, and after the bonus.

For the first experiment, results showed that the respondents' income level was a non-factor to the level of happiness, which was higher for those who spent money for others, compared to those who merely spent for themselves. The second experiment showed that the increase in the employees' level of happiness was not affected by the size of the bonus. However, it appeared to rise in relation to the amount of money the employees spent on others, or had given to charity, according to the Guardian.

"Most people would think that if you make more money you are going to be a lot happier," said Harvard's Professor Michael Norton. "Our results, and a lot of other people's results, show that making more money makes you a little bit happier, but doesn't really have a huge impact on you. Our studies suggest maybe that little changes in how you spend it make a difference."

The Telegraph reported that a follow-up experiment wherein the experts gave respondents either $5 or $20, to be spent the way they see fit, revealed that those who spend the money on others reported being happier compared to those who spent it on themselves. http://www.allheadlinenews.com/articles/7010405366

17. Do you think tithers are happier than non-tithers?

Science and the Bible agree: the generous prosper. It is good to be generous. Generous people are happier.

My own research supports this. Those who described themselves as very generous were three and a half times more likely to describe themselves as extremely happy.

When I asked about how much people have as a percentage and compare this with their reported happiness, the relationship was completely linear.

18. What keeps people from being generous?

"You have not lived today until you have done something for someone who can never repay you."

— John Bunyan

19. What do you want to recall from today's conversation?

20. How can we support one another in prayer this week?

12190631R00105

Made in the USA
Monee, IL
22 September 2019